BOOKS BY THEO LANG

The Darling Daisy Affair   1966
Great Men of Scotland   1958
The Border Counties   (editor) 1957
Glasgow, Kyle and Galloway   (editor) 1954
Edinburgh and the Lothians   (editor) 1952
The Kingdom of Fife and Kinross-shire   (editor) 1952
Highroad from Paris   1950
Cross Country   1948
House in Gowderdale   1947

By Theo Lang as "Peter Piper"

The Woman Delia   1957
The Corpse That Came Back   1954
Margot Leck   1947
Death Came in Straw   1945
Murder After the Blitz   1945

THE
DARLING DAISY
AFFAIR

THEO LANG

THE

DARLING DAISY

AFFAIR

Atheneum   New York

(*1966*)

Published in England under the title *My Darling Daisy*
Copyright © 1965, 1966 by Theo Lang
All rights reserved
Library of Congress catalog card number 66–18758
Manufactured in the United States of America by
Kingsport Press, Inc., Kingsport, Tennessee
Designed by Harry Ford
First American Edition

AUTHOR'S NOTE

A stack of papers lies before me on my desk: legal documents, telegrams from Buckingham Palace and St. James's, scribbled messages sent by agitated courtiers, and—most important of all—a bundle of love letters.

These are the instruments I have used to unlock the most closely guarded Royal secret of our day.

The subject of all these papers is one of the most famous women of our times: Frances, Countess of Warwick, a woman of noble birth and legendary beauty who nevertheless reached a point in her life when she was desperate for money and was prepared to go to any lengths to get it. Then began a tortuous intrigue which threatened to explode at any moment into a public sordid "Royal Scandal."

Frances, Countess of Warwick, was threatening to sell to American publishers the long, intimate and appallingly indiscreet letters of the King who had been her lover and addressed her as "my own adored little Daisy Wife."

She had to be silenced, but she was demanding

£100,000 as the price of her silence, and the fact that she was making that demand seemed even more dangerous than the publication of the letters. Never must it be suspected that "hush money" could be paid to keep a Royal scandal out of print.

Thus there began, behind the façade of London's social and Royal life, a backstairs operation to keep Frances Warwick quiet. A most bizarre assortment of personalities was drawn into the secret negotiations. Judges, distinguished lawyers and peers of the Royal Household found themselves incongruously entangled with financiers, private detectives, men-about-town and even a suspected German agent. One of the go-betweens became famous in his own right when he was charged with perpetrating a gigantic financial swindle: Clarence Hatry. And, to crown it all, there in the background was none other than that rascally womanizer and journalist, Frank Harris.

With such people involved, it seems a near miracle that the secret was kept. Yet it was. Lady Warwick *was* silenced, the evidence of her Royal love affair was buried in the archives, and the documents and the King's letters were spirited away.

Years passed. Frances, Countess of Warwick, mellowed into a renowned public figure, famous as a doer of good works and as the first Socialist peeress, so ardent in her political beliefs that she even fought an election against her kinsman Anthony Eden. She had her critics and she had her enemies, political and social, but no one ever attacked her by blurting out the unpleasant secret of her past.

The fact is no one could tell that secret fully. Not even Frank Harris—and how that character would have loved to recount it in his *Life and Loves*—could tell it. Harris, like everyone else involved in the affair, did not know the whole story. He knew only one little part of it.

Never, until today, has all the evidence been assembled in one place. Now it lies here before me on my desk. All of it. Letters from Lady Warwick's lover who became King Edward VII; lawyers' letters and affidavits; confidential reports of conferences at St. James's Palace and the Ritz in Paris; and the telegrams and telephoned messages that flew between Buckingham Palace and Windsor and the Royal Family's solicitors through months of secret agitated negotiation.

A strange chance—one of those lucky accidents which come like a rare bonus in a writer's life—first put me on the track of this buried story. A casual visit to a chalet high on a mountain above a Swiss lake, a gossipy conversation that prompted my host to drag a deed box into the light and open it, and there, stowed away amid a deposit of family papers and photographs, was a bundle of numbered envelopes. One glance at the letters and documents folded within those envelopes was enough. I knew that I had in my hands clues to a sensational story. Later, when

Author's Note

I began digging deeper into the story, I realized that the treasure trove I had uncovered was even richer than I had at first imagined. This buried evidence became a kind of Rosetta Stone with which one could translate secrets about King Edward and Frances Warwick and his other lovers which in the past no one had ever dared to tell and historians could only guess at. Here they are.

CONTENTS

(*ix*)

ILLUSTRATIONS

FOLLOWING PAGE 146

(*xi*)

THE
DARLING DAISY
AFFAIR

FRANCES CHOOSES A MAN

On the morning of June 25, 1914, Frances, Countess of Warwick, sat awaiting a visitor in the drawing room of 37 Eaton Square. She had traveled up to London early that day from her country home, Easton Lodge, near Dunmow in Essex, to conduct a delicate and crucial interview with Mr. Arthur du Cros, Tory M.P. for Hastings.

Throughout her life Frances Warwick had done many daring, unexpected and even outrageous things, but at this interview with du Cros she was to make the first open move in an intrigue potentially more dangerous than anything she had ever attempted. That was why, although du Cros had a home at Edgware and an office at 14 Regent Street, she had arranged to meet him on "neutral territory" at 37 Eaton Square. This mansion with a Corinthian façade on the south side of the fashionable square was the house Neville Chamberlain was to live in for thirteen years before he moved to Downing Street, but in 1914 it was the home of another Tory M.P., Captain George John Sandys, member for the Wells Division of Somerset.

Arthur du Cros was something of a notability in Tory circles. He was, among other things, a founder of the Junior Imperial League, that section of the Conservative Party designed to capture potential Tories while they were young and mold them into earnest and reliable party workers and Tory voters. He was the first chairman of the League's Committee. He was also famous as a Commons back-bencher for his courageous and imaginative support of modern scientific development. For instance, he had, during the years when airplanes were still looked upon merely as eccentric and unreliable novelties, forced the government to recognize their potentialities in national defense.

But on that June day Frances Warwick, herself renowned as the "noblewoman turned Socialist," was not interested in the Tory prestige or political importance of Arthur du Cros. At this critical stage in her career she was far more interested in what was his even greater importance *outside* politics. He was an industrial magnate, managing director of the giant Dunlop Corporation, a man of formidable wealth.

Frances Warwick had known Arthur du Cros for some years. Her only surviving child, Lady Mercy Marter, who now lives in Wales, remembers him well as "a dark man with a long nose" who had "a wonderful house" on the coast which "one lovely summer he lent to Mother. I recall the beautiful bathing." This was the same house du Cros later lent to the ailing George V, the king who was the principal target in the intrigue Frances Warwick had decided to initiate at the Eaton Square interview.

But Arthur du Cros was something more to Frances Warwick than a close friend who hospitably lent her his house for a summer holiday. He had become her confidant and financial adviser. He was also her creditor. On that June morning when she awaited him in the drawing room she owed him £16,000.

Nor was Arthur du Cros her only creditor. Far from it. By the summer of 1914 Frances Warwick had sailed deep into debt. On my desk is a sheet of paper—the torn half of a Paris hotel bill—which reveals the desperate plight she was in at that time. This scrap of paper is one of the documents in the cache of secret papers uncovered only a few months ago. On it Frances Warwick had attempted to jot down a rough estimate of her debts. One item in this penciled scribbling is for no less than £42,000. This was what she owed to tradesmen and Jews. By Jews she presumably meant moneylenders.

She had been battling creditors for years and had already been dragged into the courts as a debtor. In 1911 a Mr. Sturgess obtained two judgments against her for over £2,000 each, and when she paid only about £700 Sturgess took steps to enforce the judgment, with the result that in February 1913 the proud lady had to submit to the indignity of oral examination by a court official. The official's purpose was to inquire into her means, and it was apparently in the course of this examination that she divulged that certain property she possessed at Easton Lodge was already mortgaged to her creditors.

It seems that Frances Warwick's creditors were by this time well aware of her contemptuous disregard for legalities, and in an attempt to protect their cash they secured an injunction restraining her from raising money on the property. Even so, when a receiver was appointed and went down to Easton, however, the receiver found that, notwithstanding the injunction, a picture by Sargent, a Rodin bust, a car and all the silver and plate had gone. At a later hearing it transpired that Lady Warwick had sold the picture for £3,000, of which she had kept £580, having used the balance to pay off the mortgage. This resulted in a further order against her to attend interrogation.

As we shall see, Frances, Countess of Warwick, was all her life a proud and impetuous woman—a haughty noblewoman capable of facing up to courts and judges with grand arrogance and recklessly defying court orders. But during the weeks before the interview in Eaton Square even she realized she had reached a financial impasse. Her creditors were crowding in on her and she was enduring the humiliations of a common debtor. She had, in fact, suffered the supreme insult of being snubbed by a tradesman, and that in Leamington of all places, a town which in the past had always been eager to solicit the custom of the noble family of neighboring Warwick Castle. She had walked into one of the town's big and fashionable stores, intent on a spending spree. The proprietor had stepped forward to greet her and bowed. Such old-fashioned courtesy had always been his custom, and even on this occasion his refusal to allow Lady Warwick any more goods on credit was phrased in the most courtly manner he could devise. According to one of the biographers, he told her, "I am afraid, my lady, there is nothing in this store that is suitable for you to buy." We can be sure that Frances Warwick, famed for her haughtiness and imperious angers, would march out of the store proud and erect, but she would be quivering with the humiliation of such a rebuff.

By the middle of June 1914 Frances Warwick,

who claimed that as a child she had been worth £30,000 a year in her own right, found that she was almost broke. She was, in fact, in such a plight that she found it would be inconvenient to pay the second year's interest due on the £16,000 she had borrowed from du Cros. If forced to do so, she could just about scrape up enough money to pay that interest, but she needed the ready cash for other things.

She decided to try to stall off du Cros. Hoping that he might give her a few weeks' grace, she tried to "buy time" and asked her husband's agent at Warwick Castle, Mr. Godfrey Payton, to get in touch with du Cros and beg him to allow the interest now due him to be used instead to meet the demands of more pressing creditors.

This appeal was transmitted to du Cros through his solicitor, Mr. Purchase. Du Cros decided to refuse it. He had sound business reasons for doing so. He was well acquainted with Lady Warwick's extravagant way of life, and knew that she had long been notorious as a lavish spender.

For one evening party at Warwick she could splash out as much money as would have kept any normal family living in style for a twelvemonth. How much she spent on her other parties—the ones that lasted whole weekends or through the Christmas season—no one could calculate, least of all Lady Warwick. She was also given to sudden expensive whims. Such as, for instance, buying a baby elephant brought to her door by a traveling showman and, having bought it, starting at Warwick Castle a private zoo for which she later bought two emus which were seen early one morning chasing one of her houseguests, a gaitered bishop, through the shrubbery of the grand gardens.

Certainly such eccentric extravagances could have little appeal to a businessman like du Cros, a man who had created his vast fortune by commercial vision, a genius for investment and a due regard for the sacred dignity of money. So far as he was concerned, the £16,000 loan to Lady Warwick was a normal straightforward investment. When she had asked for it two years before, he had taken the precaution of lending it to her and to the Earl jointly on the firm security of the valuable Warwick estates. He saw no reason why he should forgo his dividends, and he was pretty sure that even if he did so, the ready cash thus made available would be swallowed up without trace in the improvident and colossal housekeeping expenses at Easton Lodge or Warwick Castle. Or perhaps—and this seemed even more likely—it would find its way into the till of her favorite dressmaker, Worth.

So du Cros instructed his solicitor to refuse her request to use his money for her own comfort. Accordingly, Mr. Purchase sent her this telegram:

ARTHUR DU CROS ABSOLUTELY DECLINES TO ALLOW ANY PART OF DIVIDENDS TO GO TO CREDITORS.

The telegram was addressed to Warwick Castle. On that day Lady Warwick was down at Easton Lodge, but Godfrey Payton telephoned the news to her from Warwick. The curt message affected her violently. So, at least, she says. Considering the enormity of her other debts and the general seriousness of her financial position, this little reverse about a few pounds of interest seems negligible, yet she claimed later that du Cros' attitude destroyed any hopes she had entertained of staving off financial disaster and social disgrace.

What she felt that morning at Dunmow is dramatically illustrated by a comment she later scribbled on another of the documents in the dossier. The telegram made her decide to see du Cros at once. He had, she argued, brought her face to face with disaster.

Disaster? Du Cros later maintained that Lady Warwick was grossly exaggerating the situation. He was not, he said, demanding the immediate repayment of the £16,000 principal: he was merely protecting his dividends. But Lady Warwick had her own devious reasons for insisting that he had precipitated a crisis. She had to pretend that she saw herself being pushed into bankruptcy, her home sold, and her style of living stripped to the bone. Then she could plead that fear of such a disaster was the only thing that had forced her into the plan she intended to put before du Cros during the interview at 37 Eaton Square. It was a possibly dangerous plan. It was certainly distasteful. But she could always say that du Cros had made it inevitable.

That is not true. Long before she got du Cros' telegram she had been contemplating the one great coup which could free her from her financial worries. The evidence now uncovered establishes that she had been brooding over this plan for weeks, possibly longer. She had one asset which, she felt certain, would realize enough to pay all her debts at one go. That asset was the bundle of love letters written to her by King Edward VII, who, when he was Prince of Wales, had been her lover for nine years.

She was right in thinking those letters could be worth a lot of money, if considered as nothing more than a titillating record of yet another of Edward's love affairs. But their value was more than that. Those long intimate letters to "my own lovely little Daisy wife" were more than concoctions of sweet endearments. They were also full of Court gossip, their pages spattered thick with the names of the highest in the land and reports of gay goings-on at such places as Chatsworth, home of the Duke of Devonshire, and other great country houses of Britain. Even more. Edward—either out of infinite trust in his darling Daisy or out of sheer besotted indiscretion—had not even restrained himself from referring in those letters to affairs of state and high policy.

Certainly, therefore, the letters were an asset of considerable financial value. The problem Lady Warwick faced was how to realize this asset. How could she turn the letters into cash?

She must have pondered over this problem for some time before she at last evolved her plan of campaign. Like a general, she decided to cover up her real purpose with a feint attack. She would pretend to be planning the obvious method of turning the letters into money—publishing them. But all the time she would be hoping to get the cash by a quite different method.

It was a plan of campaign which necessitated her playing a double game. There was always the danger that the lies she would have to tell might trip her up. In fact, as it turned out, they sometimes did. But she had not much to fear. She could be confident that the kind of people she was dealing with would be so anxious to keep the matter quiet that they would never think of exposing her if they found her out. Certainly the Royal Family could not do so.

So at Dunmow, with the cold douche of du Cros' telegram to enliven her, she launched her campaign.

The first thing she needed was an intermediary. She chose du Cros. He was, for reasons which become apparent as her intrigue is revealed, an ideal choice.

In fact, one finds oneself almost suspecting that perhaps her appeal to him to forgo his dividends might have been a move carefully designed to bring him into the picture. In any case, his refusal to accommodate her provided her with the alibi that acute financial distress had forced her into performing a disagreeable act.

So on Wednesday, June 24, 1914, she wrote to Arthur du Cros the letter which began the whole business.

It was a letter cunningly contrived to draw him into her plot. She was cautious, far too cautious to disclose in that letter precisely what she was threatening to do, but what she did write was enough to rouse du Cros' interest and anxiety. The letter—on pale-blue notepaper with the words "Strictly Private" written above her cipher and coronet, and covered edge to edge with her boldly beautiful script—is concocted in a style calculated to whet anyone's appetite.

It certainly succeeded with du Cros. The financier was enticed into curiosity immediately upon reading the letter. He had not heard from Frances Warwick for some time, and now he realized why she had been silent. She had been busy on some kind of literary project. Although she did not specify what it was, it seemed to concern some sensational revelations and certain letters. This mysterious work apparently had stupendous possibilities. At least Frances Warwick seemed to think so. Her plan, it seemed, was to sell the product of her labors and the letters in America, and du Cros was quite staggered by the amount she hoped to raise from the sale. £100,000! Enough to pay off all the debts, including his £16,000, that had worried them during their conferences on her tangled financial affairs.

What on earth, du Cros asked himself, was Frances Warwick up to now? He was flattered when he realized that he was one of only three friends to whom she had revealed her grand scheme, but he was alarmed by her bold confession that publication of her work would wreck her reputation and, it appeared, the reputations of other people.

Why, he wondered, was she telling him all this? He appreciated that she was doing so not merely because he, as her creditor and adviser, had a right to know about her finances, but because she considered him a sympathetic ally. Well, it was nice of this beautiful noblewoman to think about him like that. Nevertheless, the letter gravely disquieted him. He sensed something near to a threat in her warning that there was not a moment to be lost and that she must talk to him about her plan before it was too late. In fact, she was planning to go over to Paris in only thirteen days time—on July 7. That, it seemed, was the day when she hoped to clinch her £100,000 deal.

But why Paris? That was yet another thing that she did not explain in her letter. Her reason is obvious. At this stage she certainly would not dare to put into writing the name of the man she was to meet there, certainly not in a letter to Arthur du Cros. She was keeping that little bombshell up her sleeve until she had the financier in her presence.

She had said enough to bring du Cros hurrying to see her, but, having finished her letter, she apparently decided to make doubly sure that he would come. To do this, she wrote a second letter. This one also found its way eventually into the cache of documents and now lies on my desk.

This letter she sent to du Cros' solicitor, Mr. Purchase. It was designed to set that man's mind at rest. His telegram had disturbed her agent at Warwick, but she wanted to tell the lawyer that such trivial financial preoccupations were no longer of any importance because during the last few months she had been engaged on an enterprise which would sweep them all away. She urged the lawyer to seek out du Cros wherever he might be at that moment and make sure that he read the letter she was addressing to him at his Regent Street office.

She posted the letters from Easton that afternoon. Next morning she traveled up to London to await du Cros at Eaton Square.

Du Cros received the letter on the morning of Thursday, June 25. Within an hour his new 15

Napier car pulled up outside No. 37.

That new Napier was illustrative of du Cros. As he had demonstrated in the Commons, he was an enthusiast for all things modern—natural enough in one who founded his fortune on one invention, the pneumatic Dunlop tire—and he had a passion for cars. He had also a millionaire's capacity for indulging this passion and buying the best and the latest.

Nevertheless, in person he was still markedly conservative, even old-fashioned. In an age when men were rapidly becoming less formal in dress and manners he still sheathed himself in immaculate braided frock coats, and when he was shown into the drawing room at No. 37 he would naturally pay his respects to the Countess with the stilted formality of a bygone age. She, on her part, was all easy friendly charm. We know this from du Cros' own account of the meeting.

In the conduct of his business and personal affairs du Cros was as precise as he was in manner. We have reason now to be grateful for that, because his painstaking devotion to detail has preserved secrets which otherwise would have been lost and forgotten. His careful collection of every relevant document and scrap of paper, along with the detailed notes he made throughout the course of the "Darling Daisy" affair, allow us to follow the intricate negotiations step by step.

Arthur du Cros' "Darling Daisy" dossier came

into my hands by accident. While I was visiting friends in Switzerland, a conversation about family affairs prompted my host to drag out a deed box and open it. Amid family papers and photographs were a bundle of envelopes and two photographic plates. On each envelope was a summary of its contents, written in pencil in the thin spiky handwriting of Arthur du Cros. Those summaries told me at once that here, forgotten since the day when it had been cautiously buried away, was evidence of a startling unknown episode in history. Here was the full story of the most carefully guarded Royal secret of our day.

The photographic plates were of a letter sent by Edward to "My own lovely little Daisy," and one of the envelopes held typed copies of other letters he had written to her. The other envelopes revealed more treasures: lawyers' letters, affidavits, telegrams, even records of telephoned messages. For instance, one of the duties of du Cros' personal secretary at his Regent Street office was to type out and lay on du Cros' desk any telephone message received in his absence. These scraps of paper du Cros had preserved, filing them away with the rest of the papers he was collecting in the Warwick case.

Not content with collecting this material, Arthur du Cros had made it even more explicit by adding to it his own summaries of the interviews he conducted and the conferences he attended, meticulously pinning each move in the intrigue to its exact date. His summaries, apparently written while the conversations were still fresh in his mind, give us every nuance of every remark and every argument at each stage in the negotiations—as, in fact, they do for this first crucial interview at Eaton Square.

Du Cros' written account of the interview reveals how relaxed and ingratiating was Frances Warwick on this occasion. Of course she would be. She had to make every effort to win his sympathy. She had to make du Cros really believe that to her he was just as she had described him in her letter, an understanding friend to whom she could open her heart, reveal the truth and apply for advice in her negotiations with the wicked cruel clever world.

To make sure that this interview would go as she had planned, she faced a delicate problem of tactics. She needed to edge du Cros toward a certain decision, but she must do so without his realizing it. For the purpose of her scheme it must appear to du Cros that it was he who would make the decision, not she. In short, her task was to outwit an astute politician and clever financier by playing the part of an innocent, even rather stupid woman so distressed by financial worries that she needed the advice of a dear trusted friend.

In the playing of such a part she was helped by one aspect of du Cros' character—his fondness for a pretty woman. Tetchy and domineering as he could be with his business and political associates, he could never be so with a presentable woman, particularly when that woman was of noble birth and high title. His brusque telegram shows that at third remove—through his solicitor and her agent—he could be intransigent on financial matters. But face to face with beauty in distress he could not be harsh. I have learned enough about him to know that he would reveal this susceptibility of his at the very onset of the interview.

She had beside her a folder of papers. It was not a bulky pile of manuscript, certainly not indicative of months of work, but she had placed it so prominently in evidence that du Cros realized these papers were to be the subject of their discussion and asked her if this was the mysterious project she had told him about in her letter.

It was, she said, a sample of it, and when he asked her what this work was she began with a cautious reply. She told him that she had written her memoirs.

To du Cros, who had hurried to Eaton Square alerted by her talk of something worth £100,000, this declaration came as something of an anti-climax. He tried to evince warm pleasure in her news, but then broke off and cast around for words that would frame his thoughts in a kindly fashion. At last he began trying to advise her not to build up her hopes too high. He referred to the £100,000 she had mentioned in the letter. That, he said, was a lot of money, and honestly he could not see her memoirs— with all due respect, of course—making as much as that.

She then told him: "Some American publishers are interested in my book."

Of course. They would be. Her name and title made their interest inevitable. But £100,000! Any book would have to be a sensational success to make even a quarter of that.

But, she argued, that was just what her book would be. In fact, it could be worth more than £100,000.

Had the publishers told her that?

"No, Mr. Harris has."

Frank Harris?

She nodded.

Her bombshell had burst. Du Cros must have had difficulty in containing his anger when he realized that she had been negotiating with Harris, and Frances Warwick must herself have known full well how fiercely the very mention of the name of Harris would affect du Cros. She could not, as later events to be recorded in this history of the "Darling Daisy" affair will prove, have failed to know that du Cros had at one time been closely associated with Harris.

That association had begun in 1896 when Harris met Mr. Ernest Hooley, a financier and promoter of the Dunlop company. Harris told later how, at

Hooley's hotel, he met "Arthur du Cros (managing director and deputy chairman of the Dunlop company) who had more to do with the successful Dunlop promotion than any other member of his family and who afterwards became Member of Parliament and was knighted, I believe, for this achievement." He added a condescending description of du Cros as "an alert, intelligent man, a good organiser, but intensively combative." According to the du Cros family, Arthur du Cros actually employed Harris to write his speeches and political broadsheets, or at least edit them for him, but that was in the days when Harris had the reputation of being a forceful journalist and had his finger in every pie—in society, in finance and in publishing. By 1914, however, the former editor of the *London Evening News* and the *Saturday Review* was a suspect figure. Many years were still to pass before he exposed himself in the book for which he is most famous, *My Life and Loves*, but even in 1914 the excesses of his "life and loves" were catching up with him, and gossip about his scandalous amours had become so fierce and rumors of his increasing debts so current that he had sneaked away from the London scene and was spending much of his time in Paris. In Vincent Brome's biography of Harris the foreword bluntly states: "Harris can be described as a person who became a blackguard of the worst possible kind and who would, whatever the society into which he was born, have remained true to his blackguard's nature." Those caustic words were published in 1959, but even as long ago as 1914, when Frances Warwick mentioned the name Frank Harris in the drawing room of 37 Eaton Square, du Cros would have endorsed them, for his sons tell me that whenever he referred to Harris, which he avoided doing if possible, he always described him as "that poisonous person."

We can therefore appreciate how disturbed and shocked he was when Frances Warwick told him that it was to see Harris that she was going to Paris.

What precisely had Harris to do with her book? du Cros asked.

She explained that Frank Harris had been collaborating with her in the writing of it. Du Cros expressed his regret, adding that had she asked his advice earlier he would have warned her that the less she had to do with that "poisonous person" the better. Had she, he asked, been paying Harris for the work?

Not yet, she told him. Surely du Cros knew as well as anyone that she was not in a position to pay anyone anything at this moment—not with her finances as they were.

Du Cros could not believe that Harris would work for nothing. Surely he expected to get something out of it?

Yes. She had given him a financial interest in the project.

How much?

"Five thousand pounds and a percentage of the royalties."

Five thousand pounds! Du Cros was shocked, and showed it. He was now convinced that Frances Warwick was being cheated in typical Frank Harris fashion. As he saw it, she was doomed to pay the rascal £5,000 for working on a book which might well turn out quite worthless. What possible hope had she that the book would earn even enough to pay Harris his £5,000 fee?

Lady Warwick had no such fears. Harris, she said, had assured her that the book would probably earn at least £125,000.

So he would, thought du Cros. Harris would say anything for the sake of a sure £5,000.

The time had now come for Lady Warwick to bring the interview to its crucial point. She opened the file of papers. The book, she said, would be of particular value because it would contain certain letters. They were love letters written to her.

She drew out a letter and passed it over to him. It was addressed from Chatsworth. It began:

My own lovely little Daisy,
It is difficult for me to describe how touched

*I was by your beautiful letter which reached
me this morning which crossed mine from Sandringham which will have reached you today.*

I gave it to the Princess to read. . . .

Du Cros read only this beginning of the letter
before, with a sudden shocking suspicion, he turned
to the end of the letter. There he read, "Forever
yours, Your only love."

He looked up from his reading. Was this letter, he
asked her, from King Edward?

Yes. It was a letter to her from "dear Edward."

She stretched out her hand for it. There was no
need for him to read more. He had seen enough for
him to realize just why her book could be a sensational success.

He remarked that the letter was not signed "Edward."

That, she said, was hardly important. Her Royal
lover, who addressed her as his "Daisy wife," had
been content, and maybe proud, to sign himself
merely "Your only love." In any case, the things
he so indiscreetly and recklessly wrote about in the
letters could have been described by none other than
King Edward: the hasty angular handwriting was
unmistakably his.

When he later recalled this moment of the interview, du Cros remembered that he sat silent for a
while, trying to assess the position and to decide

what to say. Frances Warwick, we can guess, also
sat in silence. Certainly she would not want at this
stage to interrupt du Cros' thoughts, for the scheme
that she had in mind depended on those thoughts
pursuing a certain course. When he at last asked
her if she had the originals of the letters, she must
have felt that her plan was working and that the
interview was progressing along the desired lines.

Yes, she had the originals. No, Frank Harris did
not have any. Du Cros was relieved to hear that.

Mr. Harris, Frances Warwick went on, had seen
the letters, of course. A friend of hers—a dear
friend whom she could trust, she told du Cros—had
taken them to Paris for her. Then, as though acting
on a sudden impulse, she opened the file, sorted
quickly through the papers and drew out another
letter.

Here, she said, was another of the originals. She
handed it to du Cros. If he had any doubt as to the
authenticity of the letter, he could easily have the
handwriting verified.

He took the letter. No doubt he reached out for it
eagerly, so eagerly that she must have felt sure that
at last du Cros had reached the decision she had
wanted him to reach.

"Do you want me to treat this matter as utterly
confidential, Lady Warwick? Something between
only you and me?"

Of course she did not. It was of supreme impor-

(*25*)

tance to her plan that the news of what she was threatening to do should reach the ears of certain interested personages. But she did not, of course, say this to du Cros. Instead she said it was now a matter of indifference to her whether he treated it as confidential or not.

"After all," she added, certainly with a grandly casual air, "the book will soon be on the market."

"I hope not," he said as he folded the letter carefully and slipped it into an inside pocket. "I hope not for your sake, Lady Warwick, and for the sake of your family."

At this stage she would emphasize her innocent incompetence, would sigh and look sad and beautifully helpless. "I have considered all that, Mr. du Cros. But I cannot draw back now. I am determined to rid myself of debt. I have suffered worry enough for years. If I accept the American offer, I shall be free of that worry. Compared with that, nothing else matters."

"You are wrong, Lady Warwick," du Cros argued. "Something else does matter. There are greater considerations. There are the interests of the Royal Family and the nation to consider."

"I have thought of that, Mr. du Cros," she said and chose this moment to introduce into the interview another point of view. It was necessary now to make the argument which could in some measure justify what she was doing.

The Royal Family and the nation should also consider her. She was in the desperate financial position she was in today because of "dear Edward." After all, if she now made some profit out of his letters, it was only, in a way, payment of a debt. His love for her had cost her a great deal of money. Entertaining Edward was enough to ruin anyone.

Du Cros realized that at this point he could go no further in his talk with her and told her that he must have time to think over the matter.

There was not much time, she said. Her creditors were not prepared to wait much longer.

Yet it would, he said, be wise for him to consult someone about it.

"As you wish," she said. She spoke as though indifferent about what he would do or whom he would consult, but almost certainly when the door of No. 37 closed behind the departing financier that haughtily beautiful face relaxed into a smile.

The interview had gone just as she had hoped. Her plan was working. She knew precisely what Arthur du Cros intended to do with the letter he had folded so carefully into the inner pocket of his frock coat. She also had a shrewd idea whom he would try to consult.

From 37 Eaton Square, Arthur du Cros drove immediately to his office at 14 Regent Street. Alone in his private office, he read slowly and intently the letter that Frances Warwick had given him.

It was, he was later to learn, one of the shortest letters Edward ever wrote to his "darling Daisy." It was also much less of a love letter than any of the others, containing fewer endearments. Frances Warwick had plucked it from amid the others as though haphazardly taking up the first letter that came to hand, and had tossed it across to du Cros for no other purpose, she claimed, than to give him the opportunity of authenticating Edward's handwriting. But actually she could not have chosen a letter more suited to help her in the double game she was playing. This letter was undoubtedly the most powerful card in the pack. It was a loaded document of peculiarly nasty significance.

Arthur du Cros began to realize this when the name "Marcus B." in Edward's handwriting caught his eye. This could mean no other than Lord Marcus Beresford, a famous figure on the Turf who had been for twenty years manager of Edward's racing stud at Sandringham and later served King George V in the same capacity and also as an extra equerry. Edward's letter went on to refer to Lord Marcus' "Brother C."

Like most men of his time and generation, he had heard some whispers about the "Beresford scandal" in which Edward had been implicated when Prince of Wales. Certainly he realized that the letter Frances Warwick had tossed with such apparent carelessness to him was a dangerously explosive document, and this realization is certainly what induced him, before he made his next move, to take the precaution of having the letter photographed. These photographic plates are the ones I found in the "Darling Daisy" dossier in Switzerland. They lie before me now. Let us read the letter first, and then consider its sinister implications. I present it exactly as written, with Edward's uncertain punctuation and exclamation marks.

It is written on the notepaper of the Marlborough Club, that club which Edward himself founded at 52 Pall Mall when, becoming bored with what he considered the stuffy conventionality of White's and the committee's refusal to allow him to smoke in the morning room, he decided to set up a rival West End haunt of his own where he and his cronies could drink, dine, gamble and smoke to their hearts' content.

He dated the letter "Thursday evening, June 17th" without putting the year. But the year is easy to establish: it was 1897, the year when his horse Persimmon cantered home to win the Ascot Gold Cup by eight lengths, a Royal triumph which he refers to in the letter, and a triumph which, incidentally, darling Daisy had witnessed with him from the Royal Stand, where he was entertaining also Prince and Princess Charles of Denmark and Grand Duke and Grand Duchess Serge of Russia.

My own lovely little Daisy,

I lose no time in writing to tell you of an episode which occurred today after you left— wh. was unpleasant & unexpected—but I hope my darling you will agree that I could not have acted otherwise, as my loyalty to you is, I hope, a thing that you will never think of doubting! —Shortly before leaving Ascot today, Marcus B. came to me, & said he had a gt. favour to ask of me—so I answered at once I should be delighted to grant it. He then became much affected, & actually cried, & said might he bring his Brother C. up to me to offer his congratulations on "Persimmon's" success. I had no alternative but to say yes. He came up with his hat off, & would not put it on till I told him, & shook hands. We talked a little about racing, then I turned & we parted. What struck me more than anything, was his humble attitude & manner! My loved one, I hope you won't be annoyed at what has happened, & exonerate me fr. blame, as that is all I care about! How I wish "Lucknow" had won! but he really was second & the winner was most unexpected at 20 to 1. It was nice seeing just a little of you, my sweet love, & I was so happy that you could at last see a horse of mine win a great race. Everybody was most kind, & I have been inun-

dated with Telegrams & Letters! Just returned from seeing "Lorenzaccio" at the Adelphi in wh. S. Bernhardt acted wonderfully, and I think the Play would interest you.

Tomorrow I go to the Races for the last time. I have 2 horses running—but I fear they are not any good. Don't forget my darling to expect me fr. 5 on Sunday next. I only wish it could be before, but alas! tomorrow & Sat. it would be impossible——

Goodnight & God keep you, my own adored little Daisy Wife.

For ever yours,
Your only Love.

The Beresford scandal had happened before the Irish-born du Cros came to live in England, and consequently he did not know the intimate details. But neither, in those days, did many other people. Desperate efforts made by the Palace and the Prime Minister of the day, Lord Salisbury, had succeeded in keeping it from blazing into public knowledge.

In 1914, when Edward's Beresford letter fell into Arthur du Cros' hands, Lord Charles Beresford, son of the fourth Marquess of Waterford and a onetime Lord Commissioner of the Admiralty with a distinguished Naval career and honors for bravery in battle, was a fellow M.P. of du Cros', being Tory Member for Portsmouth. He had to a large extent lived down his reputation for having been the central figure in one of the nastier scandals in King Edward's checkered past.

That scandal, as King Edward's scandals usually did, involved a woman. The woman in this one had been Frances Warwick. For Frances, before she became Edward's "darling Daisy," had been Lord Charles Beresford's mistress. This was why the letter Frances Warwick had handed to Arthur du Cros apparently so casually was actually the one letter most clearly illustrating the damage she could do by publishing Edward's correspondence.

No member of the Royal Family—for that matter, no member of the government nor any person concerned with the prestige of Royalty and the good name of Britain—could fail to be alarmed at the prospect of that letter being published in America and read throughout the world. Its publication would revive a scandal that had almost lost Edward his wife, Alexandra, and might indeed have lost him his throne as well. It had needed the united power and combined efforts of government and the Royal Household to hush up the affair and keep it secret.

There are three specific reasons why this letter was indeed the trump card in Lady Warwick's game.

One: The Beresford scandal was remarkably similar to the scandal she was now threatening to unleash. The Beresford scandal had also concerned a letter, and the danger in the Beresford affair had been the same as in the threatened Lady Warwick affair—the danger that a Royal misdemeanor might become public knowledge.

Two: The letter which lay at the core of the Beresford scandal was written by Frances herself, at that time the recently married wife of Lord Brooke, heir to the Earl of Warwick.

Three: The attempt to suppress that letter was what first brought Edward and "darling Daisy" together in near-illegal collaboration, and it was presumably during this intrigue that they became lovers.

In the course of years some discreetly worded references to the Beresford scandal have crept into print. Histories, memoirs and Edwardian biographies have touched upon it. But now that the evidence of the Lady Warwick affair lies before us, the story can be seen and told for the first time in its full significance. Now at last we can see clearly how and why a lovely aristocratic and undeniably desirable woman could progress step by step, lover by lover, bed by bed, through society to become at last a Royal "favorite" and eventually reduce herself from the position of one of the wealthiest women in the land to one so burdened with debt that she was prepared to sell the secrets of her bed and the written indiscretions of her Royal lover. The story casts a livid and revealing light on the world in which Edward and his "darling Daisy" cavorted along with the Beresfords and scores of others of noble name and ancient family, and shows us just what Arthur du Cros had to face when he was sucked into Frances Warwick's money-raising scheme.

FRANCES BECOMES
"MY ONLY WIFE"

During the years du Cros had been acquainted with the Warwicks he had of course been aware that Frances Warwick's name had at one time been linked with King Edward's, but, like most people, he had not attached undue importance to that. Because of Edward's way of life and his notoriety as a womanizer it was inevitable that gossip would steam around any beautiful woman in the Royal set, and by the time Arthur du Cros settled in England the whispers about Frances Warwick seemed no longer scandalous—did no more, in fact, than invest her with a kind of romantic aura as one of the recognized beauties of Edward's circle. The letters she had shown to du Cros, however, made it all startlingly different. "My own lovely little Daisy Wife . . . Your only Love." Those endearments and the other phrases in the letters could not be explained away as sentimental half-believed rumor: they were harsh scandalous fact, establishing beyond all doubt Edward's adulterous love for a married woman.

In our day we have grown accustomed to read court reports of sexual infidelities among such people. In Edward's day one did not hear about such things. Certainly they rarely reached the courts. To the Edwardians divorce was something which was just "not done." It was unmentionable and disgraceful. It was, in fact, almost unsporting, for in the "high society" which Edward dominated for close on half a century cuckolded husbands and complaisant wives accepted almost as a kind of social convention adulterous pairings-off such as nowadays would automatically send the offended spouse screaming to the divorce court. When the heir to the throne was involved, it was even less likely that anyone would even dream of going to law. In such a case loyalty to the Crown and protocol alike demanded that there should be not one murmur of complaint. In fact, a husband might think it an honor—in any case, it might easily lead to a title or position at Court—if his wife should be accepted as Royal favorite.

By virtue of his position as Prince of Wales and future King-Emperor, Edward was naturally surrounded by noble courtiers—men and women of aristocratic lineage whose only occupation in life was to dance attendance on him and jockey for position around the throne. But Edward added to this ennobled circle other intimates more particularly appealing to his robust tastes and raffish way of life: sportsmen, gamblers, jockeys and actresses, as well as the new millionaires being thrown up by the explosive expansion of industry and commerce and the gold and diamond mines of South Africa, a gaudy gang who used an underworld of clubs and smart hotels and town houses and country seats as a luxurious warren for their pleasures, and who were at all times dotingly subservient to their social boss, the paunchy Royal with the face of a Tudor, the guttural voice of a German and the manners and habits of a Sultan. Such an atmosphere was a natural hothouse in which any woman as young and lovely and wealthy and sexually desirable—as well as sexually desirous—as "darling Daisy" would inevitably rise to the very height of social eminence: the Royal bed.

As a girl, Frances had met one of the women who had risen to the rank of Royal "favorite": in fact, the very one she herself later succeeded in Edward's affections. She had gone to the studio of the artist Frank Miles, who was doing a pencil drawing of Frances, and there saw Lily Langtry, the famous "Jersey Lily." Frances' stepfather, the Earl of

Rosslyn, invited Mrs. Langtry to dinner at his town house and eventually to Easton.

But, as a matter of fact, Frances had been chosen for a Royal bed when she was only fifteen—though, as the choice was made by Queen Victoria, the bed was of course not Edward's and certainly not an adulterous one. This was when Queen Victoria planned to marry her into the prolific Royal Family. So in fairness to Frances it can perhaps be argued that the social ambitions which years later landed her in the corpulent and whiskery embraces of the Royal Edward were probably implanted within her at an early impressionable age. The plan for this Royal alliance was born on the occasion of Frances' first visit to a London theatre, the Lyceum. There must have been some significance in the fact that the play was *Romeo and Juliet*, acted with sumptuous passion by those two luminaries of the English stage, Henry Irving and Ellen Terry.

Her host was Benjamin Disraeli, Lord Beaconsfield. Old, asthmatic and heavily rouged, Disraeli had by that time entered the last stage of his gaudy career, but, although sunk deep in voluptuous dreams of Empire, he remained sentimentally romantic, still adhering to the belief that bed was the best place for cementing those unions which lead to political, social and Royal advancement. Such a sentiment was natural in one who himself had bought the first step for his climb to political power by surrendering a delectable girl mistress to an aged Tory patron. Now, in the grandeur of age, he had turned away from the vulgar brawl of domestic politics, though he still enjoyed the position of trusted whispering confidant of his doting Queen and loved to think that he still had power to mold the future pattern of the Royal House he had helped to fashion into an Imperial one.

So, as he ran his old eyes over the fresh-complexioned radiant-eyed fifteen-year-old girl now leaning on the velvet-padded balcony of Baroness Burdett-Coutts' theatre box and thrilling to the transports of Juliet, Benjamin Disraeli began dreaming. He took the first opportunity of reporting his dreams to his Queen.

"She is lovely," he told Victoria. "Quick, intelligent and possessed of a graceful manner." Her family? "Irreproachable, one of the oldest in the land." When, in 1929, Frances Warwick did at last publish her memoirs—though *without* Edward's letters and with only an ambiguous reference to their close friendship—she opened the book, *Life's Ebb and Flow*, with the claim that she was descended on one side from Nell Gwynn and on the other from Oliver Cromwell. Her family tree showed on one side Sir Henry Cromwell and on the other "Old Mother Gwynn," who died drunk in a ditch near the site of Buckingham Palace.

But of more direct interest to the Royal matchmakers were her nearer antecedents. Her father was the Honorable Charles Maynard, son of Viscount Maynard, descendant of the Sir Henry Maynard to whom Queen Elizabeth I had granted lands in Essex. The Maynards had estates also in Leicestershire and Northamptonshire. Her mother was a Fitzroy, "doubly descended from Charles II" through the Dukes of Grafton and the Dukes of St. Albans. After the death of Frances' father, Charles Maynard, her mother had married the Earl of Rosslyn.

But Frances was a good match not only on account of her family. She was wealthy too. When she was only three she had inherited the great house of Easton Lodge, near Dunmow in Essex. Her grandfather had made her the chief beneficiary under his will and she was thus rich in her own right.

I am indebted to Mr. William Rees-Mogg for pointing out: "Her own account is that the estate amounted to 30,000 acres and in another place she refers to a revenue of £30,000 as though it might be a correct estimate. In fact the two fat folio volumes of *The Return of Owners of Land,* 1873, show the executors of Lord Maynard held at that time a total of 13,844 acres with a gross rental of £21,102. The value of the estate may subsequently have been increased by development of land in the area of Walthamstow." In 1939 Easton Lodge was described as standing in a square mile of parkland.

So she was obviously well-born enough and rich

enough to be considered a good match for Royalty. Just the kind of bride, in fact, that Victoria's youngest son, the thirty-year-old Prince Leopold, Duke of Albany, needed. Discreet hints were dropped in the direction of the Earl and Countess of Rosslyn, and just before Frances' eighteenth birthday her mother told her that the family had been commanded to dine and sleep at Windsor. Victoria had taken heed of Lord Beaconsfield's advice and was now intent on seeing the chosen bride of her Leopold for herself. The examination took place after dinner. By closely questioning Frances on her tastes in music and drawing and asking her about her ideas for the future, she put the girl through her paces. All went well. Victoria approved of the rather too vivacious but undeniably charming seventeen-year-old. The thirty-year-old Prince Leopold was therefore commanded by the Queen his mother to call on Frances Maynard.

There was, however, a flaw in Victoria's plan. Leopold had already made his own choice of a possible bride: he had fallen in love with Princess Helen of Waldeck-Pyrmont. This was something which Victoria would be the last person to be aware of, and perhaps be the last person to think it was of much account when the advantages of a Royal marriage were being assessed.

So Prince Leopold's love affair might have gone sadly for him if Frances had at that time been concerned only with the social grandeur of marrying a

Prince. Fortunately for him, however, Frances at seventeen had reached that stage in her development when a man's physical charm was more important and more attractive to her than his title, and Leopold probably saved himself from a loveless marriage by the fact that when he, obedient to his mother's command, went to pay his respects to Frances he took with him a stalwart and presentable equerry.

Frances did not think much of the Prince. He was charming, he loved music and was of the Blood Royal. But he was rather delicate and reserved, somewhat like his father, Prince Albert, and altogether too sedate for a hot-blooded seventeen-year-old. The equerry was different. Francis, Lord Brooke, heir to the fourth Earl of Warwick, was a fine upstanding man of military appearance, powerfully handsome, altogether more masculine and virile than the gentle Prince, and six years younger into the bargain. Frances, decorously entertaining her Royal visitor and intended suitor, allowed her smile to wander in the equerry's direction. She won complementary glances from him.

She had chosen the man she wanted to marry, and in 1881 the pretty twenty-year-old heiress was married to twenty-eight-year-old Francis Richard Charles Guy Greville, Lord Brooke, in the Henry VII Chapel of Westminster Abbey.

The ceremony was described as "the most brilliant wedding of a dozen seasons." Inevitably, it was attended by a clutch of Royalty. No fewer than ten members of the Royal Family were in the congregation, and on the day after the wedding Lady Brooke was commanded to dine with the Queen at Windsor wearing her wedding gown. Prince Leopold, who had so kindly helped to bring the marriage about, was given the honor of being best man. Frances later did the Prince an even greater honor: she gave the name Leopold to the first son born of her marriage.

The marriage register was signed by Prince Leopold's eldest brother, Edward, Prince of Wales, the man who seven years later was to become her lover. The heir to the throne, who attended the ceremony with his lovely wife, Alexandra, former Princess of Denmark and now Princess of Wales, was then forty, just twice as old as Frances. He was already stout, already the subject of gossip, already renowned for his gay way of life and varied loves.

The brilliant wedding, her wealth and her Royal connections launched Frances into society in grand style; her beauty ensured that she would soon be one of the brightest stars in the "Marlborough House Set," that luxurious social crowd of the titled and wealthy who dined and wined and danced and hunted and horse-raced with Edward. The highest social honor of all was to be invited to what were known as the "small evenings" at Marlborough House. These "small evenings" were not the big formal dinner parties over which Edward presided in state with his wife and which ended decorously with a ball or whist. At "small evenings" young men tobogganed down the stairs on tea trays, the rugs were pushed aside for impromptu dancing, and the exquisite wit of the brilliant Royal set was demonstrated by such elegant jokes as pouring medicinal concoctions into the wineglasses of unsuspecting guests, mingling squares of soap amid the cheeses, or topping sweets with "whipped cream" made of soapsuds. As the fun waxed, guests dueled with jets of soda water from siphons. And so on until dawn.

Amid this jolly Marlborough House mob of Royalty and nobility, Frances enjoyed the companionship of such fabulous social figures as Alfred de Rothschild, who, like an eighteenth-century Prince, maintained his own orchestra at his country seat, and Lady Florence Dixie, who walked her pet jaguar in Kensington Gardens. It was a gay amoral crowd in which a woman could indulge in the most flagrant adventures without risking being socially shunned. One woman, for instance, made a wager that she could seduce a young unattached male who had taken her fancy. The intended victim was Sidney Greville, youngest brother of Frances' husband, who was at one time equerry and part-time secretary to Edward and later private secretary to Queen Alexandra. The woman making the wager was such a ravishing beauty that everyone was sure she would easily win her bet. But she confessed, amid gales of friendly laughter, that Greville had been unmoved by her advances, had timidly taken her by the hand and led her to the front door.

The love affairs indulged in by the men and women of this giddy gang were staged for the most part in the great country houses of the titled and the wealthy. The weekend parties held in those handsome mansions set in opulent parks resolved themselves into a kind of game of musical chairs, though played with beds and at night when the servants were below stairs. In the villages at the gates of these noble country seats local folk would see the famous folk arriving, the husbands with their wives, the lords with their ladies, all decorously paired, and might raise a loyal cheer when they spotted among the arriving guests the portly bearded figure of Edward, Prince of Wales. Those innocent country folk and the bulk of the British public who read the list of guests attending the more socially important of these gatherings had no idea that the hostess had spent many frenzied hours composing her invitation list, working out—irrespective of who was married to whom—who would want to sleep with whom, and then arranging the disposition of bedrooms and convenient dressing rooms to ensure the least discomfort and the shortest length of corridor for the changes that would be made after the port had been circulated for the last time and the gentlemen had "joined the ladies" and goodnights had been said and the couples drifted away up the grand stairway to the curtained and discreetly shadowy bedroom wings. After that any bangings of doors or creaking of furniture or shufflings of slippered feet could be put down to drafts or ghosts.

Elinor Glyn, the novelist, counted Frances Warwick as her closest friend, and it is not surprising that this romantic should find amid such society a wealth of "local color" for her sultry romances. In fact, on one occasion Elinor was herself the target for amorous advances at the Warwicks' home. Her wooer was none other than Frances Warwick's husband. At the time Elinor was a member of a large house party assembled at Warwick Castle not long after Frances Warwick's husband had succeeded to the Earldom and Frances had become Countess and chatelaine of that gloriously antique home. On the second day of her stay Elinor was reckless enough to accept, in the dusk of the late afternoon, Lord Warwick's invitation to walk with him through the shadowy quiet of a newly planted rose garden. He promised to show her some choice blooms. He stood close beside her as she bent down to inspect one particular beauty, then took her in his arms, declared that she was by far the "fairest rose" in the whole garden and began ardently kissing her. Elinor struggled. She was "saved" by the inconvenient arrival of other guests. Despite her passionate pen, Elinor was a woman of decorous disposition. Nor was she, it appears, quite so cynical about extra-marital diversions as were her noble acquaintances, and she felt that she had to tell her husband about what had happened in the rose garden. She timed her confession for the moment when, in their dressing room, he was tying his dress tie for dinner. "Did he, by Jove!" Elinor's husband exclaimed. "Good old Brookie!" And finished tying his tie.

Elinor later transmuted her Warwick Castle experiences to novelist's gold in a romance entitled *The Reflections of Ambrosine.* In this novel Frances Warwick was the prototype of Lady Tilchester, whom the heroine, Ambrosine, appalled at the promiscuous interweaving of the titled folk around her, considers the one virtuous monument of chastity in a wickedly adulterous world—until the poor girl discovers that Lady Tilchester is the mother of a child by the very man she, Ambrosine, is about to marry.

Frances Warwick was one of the people particularly chosen by Elinor Glyn to read her tiger-skin novel *Three Weeks* in manuscript. She was quite shocked by it and advised Elinor not to publish it. If she did, Frances warned her, none of her noble friends would ever speak to her again. Frances Warwick's dictum was, characteristically, that one might *do* such things, but one should not *write* about them. One should not even talk about one's own or one's friends' love affairs.

The actress Mrs. Patrick Campbell put it in a

nutshell when she said, "It doesn't matter what you do in the bedroom as long as you don't do it in the street and frighten the horses."

This, then, was the kind of society in which Frances met Lord Charles Beresford, one of Edward's companions and a lusty Irish sailor, and began the intrigue which eventually came near to losing Edward his wife and might have cost him his throne and ultimately led Edward to write that Beresford letter which Frances Warwick handed to Arthur du Cros at 37 Eaton Square.

Lord Charles' elder brother, Lord Marcus Beresford—the one who "actually cried" when Edward agreed to receive his "Brother C." at Ascot—was manager of Edward's stud at Sandringham. Lord Charles had been an even closer friend of Edward, accompanying him as his Naval aide-de-camp when he made a state visit to India in 1875. Lord Charles was a brave and resourceful sailor. He was honored for gallantry during the attack on Alexandria in 1882, when, after the softening-up bombardment of the city, he was sent ashore and "restored order with admirable efficiency, nerve and tact." He distinguished himself in later engagements on the Nile and won warm praise in the House of Commons. In 1886 Edward asked the Prime Minister, Lord Salisbury, to give Lord Charles political office, and Salisbury appointed him fourth Naval Lord of the Admiralty. Less than two years later Edward had to ask his friend to resign from the government, give up his seat in the Commons and resume active service in the Navy. The reason was increasing gossip about the Naval Lord's involvement with a married woman. The woman was Frances.

One can guess that Lord Charles and Frances first met at a house party. Probably they arrived decorously accompanied by their respective spouses, their eyes met, they liked what they saw, they walked together in a rose garden or some similar shadowy retreat, and they paired off. Anyhow we do know for certain that within weeks London gossips were whispering that Lord Charles was positively "bewitched" by Frances, Lady Brooke.

Little wonder at that. To any man of normal appetites her physical charms—embellished as they were by reckless social habits, great wealth, the friendship of Royalty and some wit—were undeniably alluring.

To begin with, she was charmingly slim. In an age when women were inclined to overpowering opulence of curves, when busts jutted like mantel shelves and thighs billowed like melons from wasp-waist corseting, Frances was unusual by virtue of an alluring slenderness. The wealth she was able to spend sumptuously on clothes and hairdressers and beauticians enabled her to transform what might have been mere prettiness into the beauty which earned her the legendary title of one of the great beauties of

Edward's circle. Her features—wide forehead, arched brows, straight short nose and the firmly molded chin that looked better over a hunting stock than it did over the Warwick jewels—were noticeably similar to those of Lily Langtry, the lovely actress whom she replaced in Edward's bed. But her expression had not the warmth and sensual languor of the Jersey Lily's. Frances was more coldly classical, skilled at disciplining her features into an aristocratic and haughty primness which, in its likeness to a cool delicate pretty flower, well suited the pet name "Daisy" which her family and friends had given to her. Yet this chilly hauteur aroused more desire than could have been aroused by blatant invitation. She was adept at directing her dark-blue eyes upon her admirers with that helpless questioning clear-eyed gaze which, by investing a woman with the aura of virginal innocence, is ever challenging to the male and inflames him to hopes of conquest.

So it was with Lord Charles Beresford. But, after tasting the joys of conquest, the Naval Lord had to disengage himself from the bewitchment. He took the prudent course of going back to ships and to his wife. For him a delicious affair was finished. But not for Frances. Whether she still desired him or whether she was merely piqued at being cast aside is uncertain. What *is* certain, however, is that a letter she wrote to him was the letter of an angry deserted lover. The letter was emotional, reproachful and, above all, outrageously compromising—just the kind of letter which, by recalling the past joys of shared passion, was calculated to rekindle desire in the departed lover. At least, that was what Lady Charles Beresford thought when, by some domestic carelessness, Daisy's letter fell into her hands. She obviously thought that Lady Brooke was still a dangerous rival for Lord Charles' affections, and felt that if her husband received any more letters like this she might lose him again. She therefore gave the letter to a solicitor and instructed him to take steps to restrain Frances from writing to Lord Charles or approaching him in any way again.

Lady Charles' choice of a solicitor was the inevitable one for a woman in her position who needed advocacy in such a case. The man she went to was George Lewis, described in the *Dictionary of National Biography* as a solicitor who gradually "obtained what was for more than a quarter of a century the practical monopoly of those cases where the seamy side of society is unveiled, and where the sins and follies of the wealthy classes threaten exposure and disaster." Though Lewis appeared in practically every *cause célèbre* in the London courts for some thirty-five years, he was particularly sought after because he was even more adept at keeping things *out* of court.

Acting on Lady Charles' instructions, George Lewis communicated with Frances. The solicitor's warning filled her with fury. The knowledge that her compromising letter had been read by her lover's wife was humiliating enough; the knowledge that the letter was now in some grubby legal drawer was altogether too much. Lady Charles had proved herself a most unsporting member of her class. To make such a fuss was not playing the game: to bring in lawyers was downright outrageous.

Frances decided to get her letter back. Lewis, of course, refused to part with it. "It is my letter," she argued, "I wrote it." He explained that she was wrong. Any letter, he told her, is legally the property of the person to whom it is addressed. Although that person cannot publish the contents of the letter—for those words are the legal copyright of the writer—the letter itself, the actual sheet of paper, remains the physical property of the person it is written to. That person can sell it, or give it away, or dispose of it in any way desired.

Therefore, the lawyer told Frances, the owner of the letter she had written was the man she had written it to, Lord Charles Beresford. He, it appeared, had surrendered it to his wife, who had now lodged it with her lawyer.

Frances refused to let such legal quibbles turn her from her resolve to get back the letter. She would show this stubborn lawyer that he was dealing with someone of importance and power. She would recruit a most powerful ally to bring this Jew George Lewis to heel. She went to Edward and asked him to help her.

She had by now been a dazzling member of the Marlborough House Set for years and was on easy friendly terms with Edward, dining regularly at Marlborough House, often meeting him at Ascot and Goodwood as well as at country-house parties and London balls. She might have argued to herself that the Prince was in any case partly responsible for depriving her of her lover, and she certainly had every reason to believe that no beautiful woman would appeal to him in vain.

In our day it is difficult to imagine anyone going to a British Royal personage on such an errand, but one must remember that Frances had been brought up in circles in which Edward was known and perhaps even admired for his reckless and unregal disregard for his position when lovely ladies were involved. At that time he had already figured in two sensational scandals.

In one of them—the Mordaunt divorce case—he had been forced to appear in court to deny charges made against him when Sir Charles Mordaunt, M.P. for Warwickshire, filed a petition against his twenty-one-year-old wife, Harriet. The petition named as co-respondents two of Edward's friends, Viscount Cole and Sir Frederick Johnstone, and "others." It was popularly believed that the "others" included the Prince himself, for in a confession to her husband Harriet had hysterically declared she had been "very wicked" with Cole, Johnstone, the Prince of Wales and others. Sir Charles claimed that in her desk he had found a series of letters and a valentine from Edward.

The action was complicated by the filing of a counter-petition by Harriet's father, Sir Thomas Moncreiffe, declaring that his daughter was hopelessly insane. Doctors were called to court to establish this, but Sir Charles brought witnesses to prove that she was in her right mind when she made her confession. One of these witnesses, a maid, said: "Sir Charles usually went out in the afternoon to his Parliamentary duties. The Prince of Wales called two or three times in 1867 at that time of the day and in 1868 more frequently. In 1868 he usually came about four in the afternoon and stayed from one to one-and-a-half or two hours. Her Ladyship was always at home and saw him. No one was in the drawing room at the time. The Prince did not come in his private carriage."

The butler gave evidence that the Prince came about once a week in 1868 while Sir Charles was "in the House of Commons or out pigeon-shooting." Lady Charles had given instructions that when the Prince called, no one else was to be admitted.

Sir Charles told the court that he had warned his wife against continuing her acquaintance with His Royal Highness. "I told her I had heard in various quarters certain circumstances connected with the Prince's character which caused me to make that remark."

In this case also, letters Edward had written became the subject of argument and gossip. How compromising were these letters? This was the question everyone was asking. It was answered when a provincial newspaper printed them in full, and they proved to be friendly letters, signed "Yours ever sincerely, Edward," but far from compromising.

As a witness, Edward put up a good show. He went through the dates of his long acquaintance with Harriet Mordaunt, his meetings with her on social occasions and his frequent meetings also with her husband.

His counsel neatly disposed of the implication implicit in the maid's evidence that the Prince had not used his own recognizable carriage when he called on Lady Mordaunt. "We have heard in the course of this case," said counsel, "that Your Royal Highness uses hansom cabs occasionally. I do not know whether it is so?"

"It is so," replied the Prince.

"I have only one more question to trouble Your Royal Highness with. Has there ever been any improper familiarity or criminal act between yourself and Lady Mordaunt?"

"There has not."

There was a burst of applause, "promptly suppressed," in court as Edward left the witness box. Sir Charles' petition was dismissed on the grounds of his wife's insanity, and the then twenty-eight-year-old Edward was able to write to his mama: "I trust that by what I have said today the public at large will be satisfied that the gross imputations which have been so wantonly cast upon me are now cleared up." On the night the trial ended he went with his wife to dine with Prime Minister and Mrs. Gladstone. Gladstone was among those who congratulated him on coming out of the affair unscathed. The public was not so easily satisfied. He was hissed at the theatre and booed at the races.

Only five years after that he was involved in another love tangle. This one was not fought out in public, but it was equally dangerous to his position and actually resulted in his challenging to a duel none other than Lord Randolph Churchill. Here also, as in the "Darling Daisy" affair, letters written by Edward to a countess were the crux of the matter. These were letters he had written to Edith Aylesford, wife of one of his close friends, the seventh Earl of Aylesford, who was known in the Marlborough House circle as "Sporting Joe."

This brawl began while Edward was in India, on that same state visit when he had Lord Charles Beresford in his entourage. With him also was "Sporting Joe," but this gentleman, so needed in India because he was adept at organizing polo and pig-sticking, was suddenly obliged to hurry back to England. News had reached him that Lord Randolph Churchill's brother, Lord Blandford, was paying court to his wife. Lord Blandford had actually moved his horses to an inn near Lady Aylesford's house and was settling down for "a season's hunting" with her. Edward was upset at losing "Sporting Joe," and when he returned to England he let it be known that he considered Blandford's act of paying attentions to "a best friend's wife" despicable and that this member of the Churchill family was a social outcast.

Lord Randolph took up the cudgels in his brother's defense. Who, he asked, was Edward to critcize anyone on such grounds? What right had he to talk about "best friends' wives"? The quarrel followed a course that was echoed later in the Beresford scandal, for Lord Randolph threatened that unless Edward relaxed his social boycott of Lord Blandford he would publish his account of Edward's association with Lady Aylesford. He had, he declared, a packet of love letters written to her by Edward. It was actually rumored that Lord Randolph had climbed through a window of her house to steal the letters, though it is more easy to believe that she had handed them to him herself. Enraged by Lord Randolph's threats, Edward sent an aide-de-camp to challenge him to a duel, and suggested Rotterdam as a convenient place for the event. Lord Randolph appointed a second, but sent with him a message that he would fight any nominee of Edward's choice but could not, of course, lift a sword against his future sovereign.

Edward calmed down. The duel idea was dropped, but he made it known that he would no longer meet any member of the Churchill family nor visit any house at which they were received. It is understood that it was this social boycott which induced Lord Randolph's father, the Duke of Marlborough, to accept the post of Lord Lieutenant of Ireland, although he had a year earlier declined Disraeli's offer of the Vice-Royalty of Ireland. He accepted now, it was said, so that he could provide a home, far from the clouds of Royal displeasure, for his son Randolph and two-year-old grandson Winston. Eight years later, when Lady Blandford divorced her husband, evidence was brought that he and Edith Aylesford had lived together in Paris for years as "Mr. and Mrs. Spencer."

Thus, in a society in which these tales must often have been recalled, it would surprise no one that Frances should appeal to the Prince of Wales to champion her in an affair of the heart. She called on him at Marlborough House. She confessed her past love for his friend Lord Charles. She told about her foolish impulsive letter and what had happened to it. No doubt she even conjured tears to those wide virginal eyes when she begged him to help her.

He was touched. More than touched. He was enraptured by this appearance in his drawing room of beauty in distress—and no doubt filled with envy of Charles Beresford, who had been fool enough to surrender such a treasure.

Legally there was nothing Edward could rightly do to get hold of the letter. But Edward, filled with desire to help this lovely Daisy, was in no mood to pay much regard to legal niceties, and he went to see George Lewis. He knew the lawyer well. Lewis had actually been his guest at Marlborough House on a night when he gave a much publicized but modest dinner, "only nine courses," to give regal recognition to the stage successes of his favorite, Lily Langtry. He was also well aware that Lewis made a specialty of clamping down heavy legal lids on the simmering stews of many a social scandal and was sure the man would be amenable to persuasion. So Edward, with outrageous and indiscreet disregard for legal etiquette, asked Lewis to show him the letter. Lewis, impressed by the fact that this demand was made by His Royal Highness Edward, Prince of Wales and destined King-Emperor, meekly obeyed this order to uncover a client's papers. Edward read the letter.

"Destroy it," he commanded.

Even for George Lewis this demand was too much. Deferentially he explained to His Royal Highness that he could not destroy the letter without the consent of his client, Lady Charles.

"I shall ask her myself, then," said Edward.

He called on Lady Charles at her town house and demanded that she, as a member of his Court and thus a woman of honor, do the right thing and destroy a document which could do nothing but harm a mutual friend at Court.

Lady Charles was made of sterner stuff than her solicitor. She flatly refused. Edward left her house fuming with anger.

He returned, however. On this second visit he was in a more persuasive mood. He begged Lady Charles to be charitable, to let bygones be bygones. He assured her that there was no longer the slightest fear that Frances would ever cause her any disquiet again.

He did not specify the grounds upon which he based his conviction. At that moment the prospect that Daisy's favors might be transferred from Lord Charles to himself may have been no more than a hope. Or could it be that she had already given her Princely champion more certain assurance?

Anyhow Lady Charles remained adamant. She still refused to order the destruction of a letter which, she argued, was her only protection against Frances and her machinations.

This was outright defiance of her Prince. For this she suffered the most extreme expression of Royal displeasure. She was no longer invited to Marlborough House.

To us nowadays exclusion from that little circle of social jollity does not seem a very heavy price to pay for refusing a Prince's demands. But it was. The withdrawal of Edward's invitations did not mean merely that Lady Charles got no more free dinners or dances at Marlborough House. It meant also that she would be automatically crossed off the invitation list of every hostess in the land. Those who competed fiercely and provided lavishly to lure the Royal presence to their homes could not think of inviting to their tables a woman from whom Edward had turned away his smile.

Today it has become almost a fashion to describe the popular public attitude toward Royalty in Britain as a blend of obsequious snobbery and mawkish adulation. But it is infinitely less obsequious and less mawkish now than it was in Edward's time. In those days the square of cardboard inviting a woman to Marlborough House was a social passport far more valuable to her than her noble name, her wealth, her honor or even, for that matter, her virtue.

How devastating Edward's social boycott could be is demonstrated by the fact that eventually it reduced Lady Charles to such misery that she put her London house up for sale and made plans to retire abroad.

But she, too, had found a doughty champion to fight her cause. Hers was none other than her own husband, Lord Charles, who, seeing Edward and

Frances now in alliance against his wife, was roused to anger by the persecution. At the time Lord Charles—Irish and hot-blooded and a Naval man into the bargain—was on the point of taking up command of a cruiser in the Mediterranean, but before leaving London he blustered his way through the antechambers of Marlborough House, stormed into Edward's presence and denounced the future King-Emperor as a blackguard and a coward. He went further: at one moment he lifted his fist as though to strike the Royal visage, but then thought better of it and strode out, threatening revenge unless Edward stopped the social persecution of Lady Charles.

It seems probable that Edward was still working hard to secure the continued help of George Lewis, for within a fortnight a guest at Sandringham, the Hon. Winifred Sturt, commenting in a letter on the motley assortment of guests Edward had gathered around him there, reported the presence of an odd fish of a lawyer, a Mr. George Lewis.

It is appropriate here to record that two years later George Lewis was knighted—ostensibly for his services in connection with the Parnell Commission—and that immediately after Edward came to the throne he further honored this loyal legal lackey by making him a baronet and three years later created him a Companion of the Victorian Order.

Despite Lord Charles' threats, Edward made no

attempt in the months which followed that stormy interview at Marlborough House to restore Lady Charles to social favor. There was little likelihood that he would. Now he could not do so without offending Frances, for she had become his precious "own darling Daisy." At last she had reached the Royal bed. She was openly acknowledged as the "favorite" of Edward, Prince of Wales, and had completely ousted the lovely Lily Langtry from that unofficial but very much recognized place at Court. Now it was "darling Daisy" and not his "Jersey Lily" whom Edward invited for country jaunts or for excursions into Bohemian London.

As for the Beresfords, they seemed finally to have retreated. Lord Charles was apparently cooling off in the Mediterranean, and it could be hoped that Lady Charles, banished from the Marlborough House Set, would withdraw decently into the background or, perhaps, be content to subside into the modest and dully respectable company of the ladies socially clustered around the Princess of Wales, who, when not attending official functions with her husband, occupied herself amid a little coterie of demure matrons. Edward and Frances, however, were misjudging Lord Charles. The Irish Naval hero was determined not to haul down his colors. His wife must not retreat. Daisy Brooke should not be allowed to get away with her triumph. The knowledge that his former lover had become the Prince's intimate companion made him even more determined not only to have Lady Charles restored to her rightful position in society but also to force Edward to throw out the usurper "darling Daisy." So when at last Lady Charles wrote telling him that she could bear the humiliation no longer and was planning to sell up in London and go into exile abroad, he was roused to renewed fury. He planned to bring the Prince to heel.

On his ship—aptly named *Undaunted*—he penned a threatening and violent letter to the Prince. The days of dueling were past, he wrote, and therefore he must use for his revenge the modern weapon of publicity. He made an ultimatum: unless the Prince restored Lady Charles to her rightful position in society, he would publish the whole sordid story.

He did not, however, send that letter direct to Edward. Instead he sent it to Lady Charles, instructing her to send it to the Prime Minister, Lord Salisbury. His hope was that Salisbury would bring the pressure of government to bear on Edward. But, he told his wife, if no satisfaction was gained from Salisbury, he would instruct her by cable when to deliver the explosive missive at Marlborough House.

Even on its own, such a threat was dangerous enough. But, as it turned out, the letter could not have reached London at a worse time for Edward— or, for that matter, at a worse time for Salisbury. That it did reach London at so critical a time may have been a coincidence; but perhaps Lord Charles had strategically timed his ultimatum to hit Edward at a moment when he was at his weakest. Anyhow the letter arrived in London at the precise moment when Edward was up to his neck in a mire of public odium caused by another scandal—and this scandal could not, like others, be hushed up, because it had already reached the courts. This scandal is the one that has gone into history as the "Tranby Croft Affair."

Tranby Croft was the Yorkshire home of a ship-owner, and Edward had been staying there during the St. Leger week. In previous years when attending that racing event he had always stayed at Brantingham Thorpe, the home of his former friend Christopher Sykes, but by now Sykes had plunged into bankruptcy through entertaining his Prince too lavishly and too long, so Edward graced Tranby Croft instead with his Royal presence.

It was a most unfortunate visit. One of the guests, Sir William Gordon-Cumming of the Scots Guards, after winning £225 during two evenings of baccarat, most of it from Edward, was accused of cheating. He had actually, said his accusers, been indulging in sleight of hand with the baccarat counters: the Royal counters at that, the ones engraved with the Prince of Wales feathers which Reuben Sassoon had given Edward and which the Prince lovingly carried around with him from house to house.

Sir William's accusers insisted that he should

there and then sign a document in which he promised never to play cards again for the rest of his life. Edward was asked—and rather recklessly agreed—to add his signature to the document as one of the witnesses, and to keep it in his possession. Sir William had agreed to write his renunciation of card-playing on the implied understanding that under a "gentleman's agreement" his alleged misdemeanor would be kept a secret, but soon after returning to London he found to his distress that the affair was already public gossip.

Here, once again, "darling Daisy" slips into the story, for she is the one credited with having "leaked" the story. She had not been at Tranby Croft. She had been invited, but the death of a relative at the last moment had made her miss the party. But it can be taken for granted that Edward's favorite would soon hear all about the affair, and she was in those days known as something of a gossip. So much so that the famous Rosa Lewis referred to Lady Brooke as "Lady Babblebrook." And Rosa Lewis ought to know. She was in a privileged position to know most of the peccadilloes of the high-society set. Rosa Lewis was the woman known as the "Duchess of Jermyn Street" because in that street she ran the Cavendish Hotel, outwardly a smart and fashionable establishment but with the shady reputation of providing in London's West End the same conveniences that its wealthy and titled patrons enjoyed in their country houses.

One thing is certain: Frances was with Edward when he heard that Sir William, humiliated to know that the story of Tranby Croft was going around London, had rounded on his accusers and was bringing an action for slander against them. The news reached Edward at a New Year party at a banker's country house in Norfolk. Among the guests were Lady Randolph Churchill and, of course, Frances Brooke. Her husband, Lord Brooke, was there as well. His presence was necessary to make "darling Daisy's" presence more seemly.

Worse was to come. To the consternation of the Queen, the government and society, Sir William subpoenaed Edward, Prince of Wales, as a witness. The Tranby Croft trial proved a worse experience for him than had the Mordaunt divorce action. The trial lasted nine days and Edward was in court through eight of them. He was badly mauled by Sir William's counsel during his examination and this time there was no applause when he finished his testimony. He was there, admittedly, only as a witness, but to the public it seemed that he, his way of life, Royalty and aristocracy were all on trial.

Sir William lost his case and had to resign his commission, and with an immense sigh of relief Edward declared that he and society were "well rid of a damned blackguard," but the trouble was by no means over.

A number of great ladies—ladies close to Queen Victoria and obviously not the kind who solicited or were likely to receive invitations to Marlborough House—appealed to Dr. Benson, the Archbishop of Canterbury, to intervene. They wanted him to put the Prince on the carpet, rebuke him for his conduct and force him to conduct himself in a manner more befitting the heir to Victoria's throne. The Archbishop backed out of that. But the suggestion may have been what gave Victoria the idea of asking her son to write a letter to the Archbishop condemning gambling as a public evil. Edward did not like that idea. Justifiably he felt that the letter would be such patent hypocrisy that the public would hoot with derision. But after a decent interval and earnest discussions between Queen and Prince and Premier and Primate a long letter was concocted in which Edward, referring to the Tranby Croft trial, told the Archbishop, "I have a horror of gambling."

This was the tiniest drop of oil on vastly troubled waters. The public exposure of the kind of life Edward and his cronies lived had given the monarchy a nasty jolt. Queen Victoria recognized the real danger. In an ominously sad letter to her eldest daughter, the Empress Frederick of Prussia, she expressed somber fears. The heir to the throne, by being "dragged through the dirt, just like anyone else, in a Court of Justice," had suffered a terrible humiliation. If he could be lowered in public esteem and despised, then, she said, "the Monarchy almost is in danger."

Then, in the middle of all this, the Beresford ultimatum dropped like a bomb on the Prime Minister's desk. Lady Charles, obeying her husband's instructions sent from the Mediterranean, forwarded Lord Charles' letter, and in a letter of her own warned Lord Salisbury that her husband had already formulated a plan of campaign. If the Prince would give him no satisfaction, he would demand to be relieved of his command and would himself come to London to organize the publicity he had threatened. He would tell everything. He would tell not only how and why the Prince had made Lady Charles a social exile, but also how he had tried to make improper use of his Royal status to gain possession of a letter written by the woman who was now his adulterous mistress. Lady Charles spared poor Salisbury nothing. If he had any doubt about the relationship between Frances and the Prince of Wales, she could assure him, on the highest authority, that Frances was Edward's mistress. That "highest authority" was Edward's own wife. Alexandra, Princess of Wales, had proved she was aware of the position by openly refusing to receive Frances Brooke.

In true Salisbury fashion, the Prime Minister tried by secret diplomacy to conciliate the warring parties. In the midst of concocting the "no gambling" correspondence between Edward and the

Archbishop, he offered to put himself personally at
Lady Charles' disposal to discuss the matter with
her, and also wrote to Lord Charles reminding him of
his position as a Naval officer and of the honor he
owed to his Queen and country. Even the Solicitor
General, Sir Edward Clarke, the very counsel who
had savaged Edward in the Tranby Croft trial, was
so aware of the far greater dangers in this affair that
he advised Lady Charles not to attempt revengeful
action against the Prince.

The only gleam of hope that Salisbury could see
was that Lord Charles was still on his cruiser in the
Mediterranean. The Premier felt that a reasonable
appeal to this gallant sailor would induce him to
conduct himself as a man of honor.

But suddenly the matter got out of hand. As with
Tranby Croft, the story "leaked," and this time the
consequences were far more devastating. Gossip
about the scandal reached Denmark, where the Princess of Wales was on a visit to her parents and was on
the point of returning to London for Edward's
fiftieth-birthday celebrations. She canceled arrangements for her return. Instead she went to the Crimea
to see her sister, the Russian Empress.

The movements of a Royal personage of such
eminence as Alexandra could not, of course, be kept
secret. It was easy to put it about that she felt it her
sisterly duty to attend the silver-wedding celebrations of the Emperor and Empress, and that alibi

was readily accepted by a public which had grown fond of the beautiful Alexandra.

But there was something which Salisbury dared not reveal. Alexandra had refused to say when she would return to England. That was frightening. If Lord Charles Beresford did carry out his threat of revealing the whole scandal, then Alexandra might find it would be too humiliating to return to her discredited husband. Should that happen, there was no saying how far public indignation would go.

Edward was saved and one Royal Family crisis averted by a most providential attack of typhoid. The victim was Prince George, second son of Edward and Alexandra. Typhoid had been a dread word to the Royal Family ever since Victoria's consort, Albert, had died of it, and when news of her son's illness reached Alexandra she immediately decided to come home. Salisbury must have breathed a sigh of relief. The spectacle of a lovely Princess hurrying across Europe to the bedside of her dangerously sick son could not have been more exquisitely timed to create a wave of public affection and forgiveness for the Royal Family. The outburst of loyal sentiment which greeted the later announcement that the Prince, nursed by his devoted mother, had recovered and was now out of danger must have comforted both Salisbury and Victoria.

Such comfort was speedily dissipated two weeks later when Lord Charles Beresford stormed angrily into London. No Royal Family preoccupations and sickbed dramas could deflect him from his desire to be revenged on Edward. Arrived in London, he immediately sent a message to the Prince demanding a straight "apology from Your Royal Highness." When no apology came he began arrangements to invite journalists to his Eaton Square house for a gathering at which, he declared, he would tell the reporters his own version of the "Darling Daisy" story.

That would surely have been the most explosively dangerous press conference London had ever known. Salisbury was forced to take decisive action. Edward had to be convinced that the Beresford affair was assuming a character which could precipitate a national crisis. With the Tranby Croft episode still fresh in the public mind, the publication of the "Darling Daisy" intrigue would arouse such public disgust that there was no saying what might happen. There was only one way out of the impasse. Edward had to go some way toward meeting Lord Charles' demands.

How, Edward asked, could this be done without humiliation to him?

Salisbury had already worked it out. It could all be settled with an interchange of formal letters between Edward and Lord Charles. These letters could be so framed as to satisfy honor on both sides. Edward agreed that this seemed the best and simplest solution, but what form should the letters take? He need not worry about that. Lord Salisbury had already composed the letters. They were ready for signature.

In the exquisitely diplomatic letter that Salisbury drafted for Edward, the Prince expressed regret that there seemed to have been some misunderstanding which had caused Lady Charles Beresford some distress, but he wanted to assure Lord Charles that he had never at any time intended to wound Lady Charles' feelings.

Edward, however, had to go one step further to satisfy the Beresfords. He had to allow them one other victory. He had to agree to exclude from Court —though only temporarily—the woman who had caused the whole row, the woman who during the course of the quarrel had become his "own lovely little Daisy wife."

THE HIGH PRICE OF LOVE

Frances had no need to be particularly worried by the exclusion from Court imposed on her as the result of the Beresford imbroglio. After all, the exile was only a formality: it meant that the names of Lady Brooke and her husband would no longer appear on the lists of those invited to Royal dinners and grand state occasions at Marlborough House and elsewhere. But those were dull affairs at which Edward would in any case have his legal consort, Alexandra, on his arm. The "exclusion" would not prevent Daisy from joining Edward on his *sub rosa* late-night jaunts into the Bohemian London of discreetly shadowy clubs and alcoved restaurants. Nor would it prevent her from meeting him along the curtained bedroom corridors of the great country houses of their friends, for those hosts and hostesses who had the honor of inviting their ruling Prince to house parties knew well enough that the Daisy who was officially excluded from Court must nevertheless be invited. Along with her husband, of course. Perhaps Frances Warwick was recalling such visits when, years later, she wrote in her memoirs an acid little comment about the *"unnecessary presence"* of Lily Langtry's "uninteresting" little husband.

It does seem that although the Beresford scandal had brought Edward near to disaster in his public life and assuredly must have been irksome and humiliating to him in his private life, it was for "darling Daisy" herself quite a triumph, and the seal was set on that triumph when she finally regained possession of the compromising letter which had sparked off the affair. The Beresford family had been persuaded to return it to Frances so that Frances herself could consign it to the flames and know it could never again be used against her. It may have seemed to her almost a pity to destroy this souvenir, the precious document which had, in a devious way, served its purpose in the grand design of her life, resulting in her cementing a liaison as brilliant as any woman in Britain could achieve. But she was well rid of the letter. It was unwise to leave a written reminder of a past love lying around, and in any case her new love affair was now providing her

with letters far more valuable than any she could
write—letters which she was filing carefully away
amid the secrets of her desk. Those letters from her
"only love" were indeed precious documents: testimony establishing that she had won the confidence
and adoration of the Prince of Wales, future King-
Emperor and dictator of society. Excluded from
Court she might be, but among the Prince's intimates
she was openly acknowledged as Edward's reigning
favorite, undisputed successor to the fading Lily
Langtry, and if ever proof were needed of that, then
here were the letters sent to his "own sweet wife."

That Edward loved Frances is beyond question.
Even if the letters he wrote to her had not now been
unearthed, the open recklessness with which he championed her cause in the Beresford affair was enough
to prove the intensity of his infatuation for her. But
the letters show more than infatuation: they show the
depths of a growing devotion. The last letters he
wrote to her, for instance, reveal that when his
physical passion for her had expired and he was
satisfying such appetites with another woman and
was raising her to the rank of "favorite," he still
retained his devotion to "darling Daisy." In fact,
two letters in which he unburdened himself to his
"Daisy wife," penned when he was staying with the
Duke and Duchess of Devonshire and early in the
morning was alone in his dressing room at the ducal
palace of Chatsworth, show Edward in a gentler

mood and a better light than the public gossip that portrayed him as a heartless profligate. Doting and appallingly indiscreet those letters seem, and one is shocked to think that a man destined to rule an empire was so ingenuous and trusting as to chatter so unguardedly to anyone, let alone "Lady Babble-brook"; yet one cannot fail to think that this ingenuousness reveals a generosity of mind, an impulsive trust in the basic honesty of anyone upon whom he had turned his affections.

Which makes all the more distasteful the other question one must also ask. Did "darling Daisy" really love him? Or, for that matter, did any one of those desirable and intelligent young women who submitted to his embraces love him? The more one searches for proof that they did, the more one is forced to the conclusion that only one woman in Edward's life had real affection for him. That woman was his regularly betrayed and persistently flouted wife. But, unfortunately, the love that dear deaf unpunctual diffident lady could give him was not the kind of love to satisfy a brilliantly lusty male. Alexandra's love was the love of a dutiful and faithful consort who had been mated to him in the callously calculated way in which Royal marriages are contrived, their purpose being to ensure that Princes are procreated only in Royal wombs and thus sustain through generations the mystique of Royal Blood. In an alliance which was not far removed from a prefabricated regal coupling, Edward could hardly hope to be met with the ardent love of an enraptured spouse, and one can understand, even sympathize with, the frustrations a well-fed sensual male of lively appetite could feel in a union which was merely a political contrivance to maintain the Royal succession. One sentence in a letter that his father wrote to Edward when a meeting was being arranged between him and Alexandra is enough to illustrate the odious cattle-breeding mentality which can govern a Royal stud. From father to son comes this cynical instruction of getting on with the job of choosing the right bride for the breeding of regal litters: "We must be quite sure, and you must thoroughly understand that the interview is obtained in order that you may propose to the young lady."

Even so, it is sad that Edward was apparently incapable of realizing that the devoted marital affection Alexandra gave him could have provided him, had he had the sensitivity to appreciate the fact, with joys far deeper and more lasting than the pleasures he "bought" from women like Frances Warwick. From those, it is deplorably obvious, he got nothing more than what many a doting middle-aged man can buy from a young mistress.

This judgment is not based merely on the gross disparity between their ages. Many women and young girls are by their psychological make-up strongly attracted, emotionally and sexually, to mature and even elderly men. If this were the condition of Frances or of Edward's other favorites, then we could see them as victims of passions so overwhelming that they could not resist the temptation. Or if we could discover in Edward as a man some traces of masculine beauty or virility or some other irresistible attraction that might sweep a woman off her feet and out of her mind, even that would provide some excuse for those women who queued up on the rungs of the social ladder to climb to the position of reigning favorite in his bed.

But nothing that any one of these women has ever said or done or written reveals any trace of such compelling desire; nothing at all disproves the disagreeable truth that they saw Edward only as a grand social catch and their bodies as the easiest snare to use for the capture.

In the mid-Victorian era, when journalists had the guts to comment candidly and honestly on the habits of even the most exalted Royal personages, one magazine published a cartoon which sums up the public view of Edward's way of life. The cartoon showed a comely girl making up for an evening out. Beside her looking glass was an invitation to Buckingham Palace. The caption to the cartoon was "She Stoops to Conquer," and on her bed lay Edward's cigarette case. Nowadays we are more polite, so that any such liaison as Edward's with "darling Daisy" must be shrouded in public print with the figleaf of timid contemporary journalism—as it was, for instance, in *The Times* obituary of Lady Warwick, where the whole of a nine-year love affair is watered down to one sanctimonious fable: "Above all she enjoyed the friendship of King Edward VII, both as prince and sovereign. . . . King Edward liked her for her wit and vivacity, and there was besides a bond of union in their interest in the common people."

When, at the height of the Beresford affair, Frances and Edward became acknowledged lovers, she was only thirty and looked younger, was undeniably a beauty and, as she seems to have been that way inclined, could easily find very personable men to engage in adulterous infidelities. For she had already proved—by her marriage to Lord Brooke and by her affair with Lord Charles Beresford—that her taste in lovers ran to men of her own age and men endowed with some measure of good looks and stalwart bodies. Whereas the Edward whom Rudyard Kipling cruelly described as "that corpulent voluptuary" was twenty years older than she and looked more, and was into the bargain heavily bearded, gross and graceless in figure. No one need think very hard to imagine the commonplace and vulgar phrase Frances Brooke and those other women would have used to describe any other man of that age and that appearance who made amorous advances to them. But because Edward was Prince of Wales they could not even think of saying such words as "dirty old man." Their intense besotted social snobbery was such that, instead of shrugging away his heavy caresses, they actually encouraged them, flaunted them proudly as though his hands had invested their flesh with Princely orders.

This is not a condemnation of Edward and his moral conduct. We know that Edward was a man of lusty appetite—nothing unnatural nor wrong in that—and he had pretty well unlimited opportunities of satisfying those appetites. Let us admit that few of us, given such advantages, would have behaved as well as he did: most of us would have behaved worse. Nor does this writer wish to appear in the guise of a tongue-in-cheek Puritan censuring the morals of the Edwardian era, for they were neither worse nor better than the morals of any other era. But what we must deplore is the candy floss of sentimental romanticism and gossip-column snobbery that was and still is puffed up around the capers of the wealthy, the famous and the titled—and even Royalty—so that marital adventures and sexual exploits we are expected to condemn when they happen in the streets of Battersea are glamorized into grand passion if they happen in Mayfair penthouses or ducal homes or palaces. This process of romanticizing is seen at its most cloying in much that was written and still is being written about Edward and his times. Seen in its proper perspective, the

"Darling Daisy" affair is a murky episode in social snobbery and blackmail, and its historical importance lies not in the entanglements of adulterers but in the fact that the personages involved were the ones a whole generation of ordinary folk were and are exhorted to look upon as their rulers and their betters.

We cannot blame Edward for taking the normal masculine advantage of what Frances Warwick offered him. Few men would have resisted the temptation of such a pretty woman sprawled in his path and awaiting his hand, particularly a man who had suffered Edward's upbringing. In recent years psychologists have taught us enough about the frustrations and repressions embedded in young people brought up in the stuffy prudishness of hypocritical Victorian homes, and we must not forget that poor Edward was not the son of just *any* Victorian home: he is the son of *the* Victorian home *in excelsis*, and his mother the most ferociously "Victorian" of all. To those in her family who meekly obeyed her, Victoria could be all bosomly overpowering affection, but any deviation from her edicts aroused her to matriarchal savagery, a savagery all the more formidable because she really believed that she did what she did "for their own good." Like all grossly sentimental and woolly-minded romantics, she was acutely sensitive to any hurts or deprivations she herself suffered, but was blindly insensitive to the hurts and deprivations she inflicted on others.

A depressing instance of Victoria's lack of compassion or understanding is seen in the revulsion from Edward she evinced when, at the age of twenty, he confessed to what was probably his first sexual adventure. It had begun in an Irish barracks. This "first love" was an actress, Nellie Clifden, whom some brother officer in the 2nd Battalion of the Grenadier Guards at the Curragh had, in an excess of hospitality, smuggled into the young Prince's bedroom. Victoria irrationally believed that the shock and disgrace of this scandal had broken the heart and hastened the death of Edward's papa, her adored Albert. Even so, any mother who could write of a son, as she did, "I never can or shall look at him without a shudder" is such a mother that in a lower plane of society we should be astonished if even one of her children failed to blossom into a juvenile delinquent.

It is hardly surprising, therefore, that when Edward reached an age when he could escape from Victoria's oppressive maudlin matriarchy he should drift into the way of life and the kind of company that attract any badly brought-up man possessed of too much spending money, no real occupation and, into the bargain, a dominating widowed mother who constantly denies him the slightest opportunity of working off his energies in "the family business."

Thus the grown-up bearded baby whose immaturity was barely concealed by the piled-up pomp and regalia of Princely title and robes and coronet was actually a pathetic sitting target for socially ambitious hostesses, and a whole pack of them vied with each other in the hope of capturing the Royal person as an exclusive trophy, each one attempting to bait her trap with titbits more luxuriously and opulently tempting than those her competitors could afford.

His strapping and voluptuous appetites set the tone of all entertaining. The dinners, house parties, balls, hunts, race-course outings and every other social occasion he honored with his presence were characterized by extravagance which reached the very heights of recklessness and Trimalchian vulgarity. Up to a dozen country houses in any given weekend would have their larders stocked with costly foodstuffs, many of the exotic ingredients imported freshly from abroad, on the mere chance that Edward, Prince of Wales, might descend upon them unannounced, as he sometimes did when driving in the country. One delicacy always kept in reserve was ptarmigan pie, a specialty of the Edwardian era which was his particular favorite as a dish and for which his appetite was exceeded only by his appetite for the more tender flesh of other favorites. On the occasions when he consented to make a formal and extended visit to a country house, some hostesses would spend frantic weeks designing and effecting new decorations and furbishings for the Royal suite, showing off their own grandeur and at the same time proclaiming their lavish devotion to their Prince by changing the whole scheme of his rooms for each and every visit.

Along with Edward a whole crowd of other guests had to be sumptuously entertained, for on his visits he liked to be surrounded with his gay fun-loving sporting cronies. Nor were the guests the only problem. Edward arrived with a retinue long enough to satisfy an Eastern potentate. He brought his own footmen to stand in the Royal livery behind his chair and serve his meals; two horses and two grooms; two loaders for when he went shooting; a gentleman in waiting; and a couple of equerries—as well as two valets, for he always traveled with so many clothes that two men were fully occupied in his dressing room. His two other valets he left at home to sponge and press the ranks of suits and uniforms of his enormous wardrobe and to keep the moths out of his collection of one hundred hats and caps. A whole wing of his host's house had to be set aside for Edward's servants.

Such opulent habits made Edward a formidably expensive visitor, and one can understand the feverish extravagance into which Frances Warwick plunged when she decided to lead the field in lavishness of entertainment for her Prince. It was a costly business, but she had to put up a show against people like the Rothschilds—such as Alfred, who had his own private orchestra—and the Duke and Duchess of Devonshire, who sometimes had up to 470 people, guests and servants, under the Chatsworth roof. Frances played the game valiantly and gave no thought either to expense or to the jingle of money streaming out of her family coffers.

A Christmas party she gave at Warwick Castle lasted three days: one night for family and friends, one night for the tenants of the estate and one night for "the poor" of the town of Warwick. A full orchestra played Gilbert and Sullivan music, a Christmas tree towering to the height of the great hall was replenished each day with costly gifts, and Frances, gloriously gowned in special Worth creations, moved through the guests accompanied by her collie, Elaine. To Warwick Edward came *sub rosa*, attending house parties embellished with "professional beauties" like Frances Warwick's half-sister, the Duchess of Sutherland.

But it was at Easton Lodge, the home she had inherited from her grandfather and where she lived with her husband before he succeeded to the Earldom and moved to Warwick Castle, that she most often entertained her "only love." He spent many weekends there. Recalling those visits, she wrote later: "How thankfully he threw aside for a few hours the heavy trappings of his state to revel in his love of

nature." She paints an idyllic picture of this nature-
loving Prince walking with her across the park of
Easton Lodge on Sunday mornings to the church
where generations of Maynard forebears lay at rest,
and the novelist Ursula Bloom, whose father, Harvey
Bloom, helped Lady Warwick with her book *Warwick Castle and Its Earls*, tells of a piece of sentimental gardening at Easton—a herbaceous border
known as "The Friendship Garden" in which were
planted only flowers given to her by friends, each one
staked not only with the name of the plant but with
that of the friend as well. Edward, as befitting a
Royal personage, formally planted trees at Easton.

It sounds all delightfully rural and peaceful, but
Edward's visits were not always so modest. Sometimes Edward wanted more sumptuous regal entertainment, and on those weekends Frances would have
to do as his other hostesses did. She had to draw up a
list of the invited guests and let him see it. He might
delete some of them or add others whom he wanted
to come down to Essex and dine in grand state with
him off Easton Lodge gold plate.

The great house, lying between Bishop's Stortford
and Dunmow, was somewhat off the beaten track
and difficult for Edward and his guests to reach. All
right then, Frances decided, she must have a railway
station of her own. She got it, and local people could
now gather there to see Daisy drive up to the station
in a wagonette to await the arrival of the special

Royal Train bringing her Prince and carriages of guests to Easton and could raise loyal cheers or touch loyal forelocks as she carried off her Princely prize to her great house for a weekend's pursuit of the joys of love and ptarmigan pie.

The spectacle of Daisy whisking Edward off from the station to her home exquisitely illustrates the real relationship between those two. It demonstrates the truth that Frances Warwick can in no way be considered as a woman of the harem carried off in the chariot of her potentate. It was the other way round. She was the conqueror, he was the captive. Hers was the triumphal procession up the drive of Easton Lodge and through the drawing rooms of London. In the social game of "hunt the Prince" she had beaten all her competitors.

As for his wife, the betrayed Alexandra whose natural diffidence was intensified by her affliction of deafness, she was no woman to put up a fight for a husband. She was merely a Princess, the consort of the Prince, to whom one formally curtsied when one confronted her encased in the arid grandeur of robes and gems and crown as Princess of Wales, and then, having performed that graceful obeisance, allowed her to fade back into the shadow suitable for a discarded wife. Years later, when Frances had become the Socialist Countess of Warwick and famous doer of good works, she wrote—the conventional sugared clichés such as one uses about Royalty dripping easily from her pen—a kind appreciation of Alexandra. But this honeyed patronage of the woman whose husband she had snatched seems more deplorable than the gossip Frances joined in during the days of her triumphant adultery, when it was whispered that Alexandra, to keep age at bay, had undergone the new beauty treatment of having her face "peeled," a process reputed to remove the wrinkling top skin and uncover the fresh smooth skin below. It is some little satisfaction to know that the gossips were saying the same thing about Lady Warwick. She too had to preserve her looks if she were to keep Edward.

After the quiet church-going weekends at Easton Lodge, Edward and his "darling Daisy" began to be seen together more and more often, more and more blatantly. She did not share his enthusiasm for horse-racing nor his obsessive ambition to achieve triumphs on the Turf, but Edward had given her a Jockey Club ticket and she enjoyed the favorite's privilege of going to Epsom on the "Royal Special."

They were often seen together also in the "after-theatre" restaurants of London. Just as his namesake and grandson, the future Edward VIII, now Duke of Windsor, was to do a generation later, Edward enjoyed dining in a casual Bohemian manner with the titled and wealthy habitués of London-by-night. One of his favorite haunts was Rules, the little restaurant in Maiden Lane off the Strand, famous for its theatre clientele. Rules, however, had only one "private room" where a gentleman might, after ample wining and dining with a fair companion, enjoy more intimate entertainment. But some other restaurants—including the Café Royal and Kettners—had several private "dining" rooms thoughtfully equipped not only with table and chairs but also with a settee. Private rooms in some restaurants were big enough to seat a dozen at the table, but at more intimate dinners a maid would slip in after the table was cleared, touch a button on the paneling and reveal an ample bed. One room on the second floor at Kettners in Soho is still known as the Edward Room.

Frances traveled further afield with Edward. International rivalries and antagonisms made him for a time unpopular in France, but, Paris being the city all lovers sought, he went there with Frances Warwick—not as Prince of Wales but as a private individual. He had taken Lily Langtry there, so he could do no less for Lily's successor. He dined her at the best restaurants, went shopping with her and, naturally, took her to the top of the Eiffel Tower.

She became his dear and constant preoccupation. The letter he wrote from the Marlborough Club on the day when Persimmon won the Ascot Gold Cup demonstrates the warm protective affection he felt for her. Knowing what we now know about the Beresford scandal, we can understand why, after

Edward had allowed "Brother C." to stand humbly before him, hat in hand, offering his congratulations, he had to write immediately to Daisy to explain how that had come about. It was late, he had had a busy day at the races and a long evening of Sarah Bernhardt at the theatre, but he had to take the first opportunity of putting "darling Daisy" at ease. For he well knew that within hours all London society would be gossiping about the scene at Ascot, and that everyone would be speculating upon the significance of Edward "receiving" Lord Charles again, actually standing chatting with the former lover and later enemy of Frances Warwick. Edward had to tell her the true story as soon as possible and express his hope that Daisy would never think of doubting his loyalty to her.

On occasions when Daisy was not with him his thoughts would often stray to her. Sometimes when he attended parties at country houses where the presence of his wife, Alexandra, was socially necessary and therefore Daisy could not be with him, he would lovingly and patiently write full accounts of all that was happening. Typical of this kind of letter was one that he wrote on a Friday morning in his dressing room at Chatsworth, the home of the Devonshires.

On Wednesday it never ceased raining, so all
ideas of shooting had to be abandoned, but some

of us took a walk after luncheon, and went to see that splendid big conservatory.

Yesterday the weather was quite pleasant, and we had a nice days shooting. After dinner Miss Muriel Wilson and Albert Mensdorff acted a short French play quite admirably. They would make their fortunes on the stage.

Afterwards Mrs W. James and Mr Leo Trevor acted a short impromptu piece. It was most amusing, as the former impersonated a little girl of twelve in short petticoats and did it to perfection, whilst the latter was got up as a school mistress and was remarkably clever.

Tonight we have "My Little Dodge," a 3 act play in which Mrs W. James, Lady R. Churchill, Mr L. Trevor, Captain Jeffcock and P. Mildmay act. Everybody seems gone mad about acting here. It is, however, a welcome change from the gambling!

We shoot again today and it promises to be fine.

Now my loved one, I bring these lines to a close, as I must dress and breakfast. God bless you, my own adored little Daisy wife. I do so hope that you are feeling better in health and spirits.

For ever yours,
Your only Love.

In another letter from Chatsworth he recalls nostalgically a previous visit when Daisy was there with him.

> *We have an enormous but pleasant party here, though everything reminds me so much of the happy days we spent here two years ago! The list of guests in the papers is correct, but Lady Randolph and Mensdorff do not arrive till this evening.*
>
> *We had some very pleasant shooting today, many rabbits and some high pheasants.*
>
> *We go to Town on Saturday till Monday, and on to Sandringham on 13th.*
>
> *God bless my own adored little Daisy wife!*
>
> > *For ever yours,*
> > *Your only love.*

Apart from the mode of address he uses, such letters merely filled with social chitchat were not dangerously indiscreet, though they did reveal the rather childish tastes of leaders of British society diverted by such things as a man dressed up as a schoolmistress and an Edwardian matron pretending to be twelve in short petticoats.

Charades were a popular after-dinner diversion at high-society house parties. Apparently Lady Warwick's literary collaborator, Harvey Bloom, was a notable performer and there is at least one recorded instance when she was making a special effort to get him to a party at Warwick Castle to play his part in the show. Edward was not ashamed of showing his pleasure in such naïve entertainments. He was honest enough never to pose as a sophisticated admirer of the arts. In fact, he disliked classical music so much that he was known to bring Royal concerts to a sudden end by standing up and marching out if Sir Walter Parratt, Master of the King's Musick, introduced it into the program. He could just about tolerate Wagner, but preferred Sousa and his band.

Some of his letters to Daisy, however, reveal something far more discreditable than a lack of intellectual appreciation. They show him as inconceivably unaware of the discretion one in so high a position of state should exercise. It is one thing for a Prince of Wales to write to his mistress about the party highjinks of his social associates: it is a far more dangerous thing to write to her on matters of national and international policies. In one letter to her, for instance, he commented upon the Russian Emperor's expressed hope for international disarmament and told his "darling Daisy" that he considered it the "greatest rubbish and nonsense I ever heard of." It is the kind of comment the heir to the throne might, under duress but in utmost secrecy, make to his Prime Minister or Foreign Secretary. But here he was writing to a notorious gossip.

Lady Warwick herself, in one of her first exercises in autobiography, *A Woman and the War*, which she published in 1916, revealed that when he came to tea with her some time in 1909 or 1910— long long after she had ceased to be his favorite— he revealed to her his admiration of the way the German people were ruled and suggested it would do Britain good to be governed by the Germans for a spell. How the writer of *Mein Kampf* or any Nazi propagandist would have relished such frank acknowledgment of Germany's political superiority from the authoritative lips of Britain's King-Emperor.

Frances Warwick, of course, gloried in being taken into Edward's confidence on political affairs. The opportunity it afforded her of retailing his privately expressed opinions on important matters of state endowed her with the glamour and importance of a Pompadour.

But such indiscretions could easily have had serious consequences. How serious is demonstrated by the diplomatic furor Edward caused when he championed his "darling Daisy" in an argument with a German ambassador. This occurred soon after the Jameson Raid. The German Emperor Wilhelm, an impulsive braggart who was as indiscreet as his cousin Edward, had sent a congratulatory telegram to the Boer President, General Kruger, and soon afterward the story was going about London that Frances Warwick had written the Kaiser an angry letter protesting against his poking his German nose into Britain's affairs. How the story got about is not known, for no such letter, it appears, had ever been sent. But it is possible that in an attempt to impress someone with her important role as Edward's confidante Frances Warwick had given the impression that she really had made such an outrageous incursion into foreign politics. However, what is significant is that when the story reached the ears of Count Munster, the German Ambassador in Paris, he believed it. He obviously knew enough about Frances Warwick, her access to state affairs through Edward, and her notorious impulsiveness to accept that she had sent the letter. Accordingly, he wrote to Lady Warwick's mother sternly rebuking her daughter's conduct, describing her action as "most impertinent" and adding, "She ought to be dressed in black and hold her tongue and her pen."

Thus attacked, Frances turned to Edward to sustain her and asked him to assist her in putting the German Ambassador in his place. Thus we have the spectacle, ludicrous were it not so hair-raising, of the future King-Emperor taking up the cudgels for his mistress against the Ambassador of a foreign power with whom at that moment, Lord Salisbury had told Edward, England was on the brink of war in South Africa. Considerations of national security or possible international conflict apparently counted for nothing with Edward when compared with the hurt feelings of "darling Daisy," and he drafted a letter for her to copy out in her own hand and send to Count Munster.

Mamma (or My Mother) has shown me your letter. Lady Warwick has not the honour of His Majesty's acquaintance and it was not therefore likely she should write to him. Count Munster should have disbelieved so palpable a lie! This is, however, not the first time you have said unkind things about me to Mamma, as a few years ago you asked her at Homburg when I was going to be divorced!

The Count sent no reply to that letter.

Playing at politics when one has the future King as one's source of knowledge was exciting fun. It undoubtedly gave Frances considerable importance and strengthened her position in society, but her friends were startled and her Royal lover bewildered when in the full flight of her social magnificence she became a Socialist. The sudden conversion of the luxury-loving "Lady Babblebrook" into a Socialist was, strangely enough, the direct outcome of her lavish extravagance as a hostess.

The story begins with the great fancy-dress ball she staged in 1895 at Warwick Castle. After a year

of mourning for the fourth Earl of Warwick,
Frances and her husband, the fifth Earl, moved into
the castle. Frances, now a Countess, planned a
sumptuous housewarming, and Warwick Castle was
certainly a magnificent setting to inspire her to
extravagance.

Warwick Castle, standing on a rock rising sheer
out of the River Avon, has been in possession of the
Warwicks since the Middle Ages and its battle-
mented walls and towers were built in the fourteenth
and fifteenth centuries, but the interior is largely the
work of Fulke Greville, who was granted the castle in
1604 by James I of England. He converted the
medieval fortress into a magnificent seventeenth-cen-
tury mansion, described at the time as "the most
princely seat within these midland parts of the
realm," with an approach cut into solid rock winding
from the porter's lodge to an outer court and an
impressive double gateway between the massive 106-
foot Caesar's Tower and Guy's Tower. Overlooking
the Avon is a block of communicating rooms no less
than 330 feet long including the great hall. The
galleries are lined with portraits of Warwicks and
past Royalties by Rubens, Van Dyck, Holbein and
Lely. Frances added two portraits of herself, one by
Carolus-Duran and one by Sargent. Among the
treasures of the castle were Cromwell's helmet, a
camp kettle used by Warwick the Kingmaker, and
the famous "Warwick Vase," a fourth-century B.C.

treasure five and a half feet high and seven feet in diameter, brought from Hadrian's Villa at Tivoli.

In a boudoir was something which possibly gave Frances Warwick the motif for the fancy-dress ball that was to be the finale of her housewarming. This piece was a clock that had belonged to Marie Antoinette, and Frances decided to stage at Warwick a *bal poudré* of staggering and preposterous grandeur.

The guests were asked to wear costumes of the Louis XV or Louis XVI period. She invited no fewer than four hundred—so many, in fact, that they caused something of a "traffic jam" at the costumers' and hairdressers' in London. As it turned out, there were not enough hairdressers in London to cope with the job of dressing and powdering the fantastic hairdos, with the result that one guest was reduced to sending to Paris for a hairdresser to come over especially to prepare her for the Warwick event.

Frances Warwick dressed, of course, as Marie Antoinette. Her gown, as sumptuously regal as befitted her now semi-regal state as Edward's favorite, was made by Worth. She had most of her gowns and frocks made by this famous couturier. A Worth frock never cost less than one hundred guineas, sometimes half as much again, which was a lot of money in those days—far more, indeed, than the whole annual income of any working-class family in Warwick or London.

Orchestras played for dancing in the state rooms, and the call to supper in the great hall was sounded by brilliantly uniformed trumpeters. The house-warming was a rousing success, for, after all, it was a grimly freezing winter and this scented and powdered event seemed a warm and glittering oasis in a Britain darkened with chilly industrial poverty. At least, that is how most newspapers reported the opulent shindig, and the illustrated society magazines were full of pictures of the eighteenth-century beauties in their crinolines and gems.

But one editor dared to protest against what he thought was an outrageous display of frippery and waste. This was Robert Blatchford, editor of a Socialist sheet, *The Clarion,* who published an article caustically attacking Frances Warwick and her class for indulging in such trivial but costly pleasures during a grim winter of unemployment and poverty. The writer of the article emphasized the reckless improvidence of the hostess, Frances Warwick, by recording that she had bought a £800 fur mantle for the occasion and then carelessly lost it in a carriage.

As ever, Frances flew into a fury at being criticized, and with characteristic impulsiveness she decided to tackle this grubby little journalist in person and put him in his place with a fine show of aristocratic hauteur. She went in person to Fleet Street and climbed to Blatchford's office on the top floor of a ramshackle building. She recalls in her memoirs: "I remember thinking that the garment he wore, which was something between a dressing-gown and a lounge coat, was most undignified."

Blatchford himself later described this interview. Even this good journalist and Socialist was sufficiently conditioned by social tradition to be impressed by the accepted legend of her unparalleled beauty, and he pays due tribute to that beauty without pausing to reflect that any woman dressed by Worth and groomed by a diligent and dexterous personal maid cannot fail to make a sumptuously desirable impression amid the inky proofs of an upstairs newspaper office in Fleet Street. Her beauty, he recalled, "was amazing and striking. I remember that the man who came to announce her arrival to me was absolutely speechless because of it. His eyes seemed to be popping out of his head."

Even so, however much the gaze of those dark-blue eyes and the curves of her slim figure impressed Blatchford, he was sincere and fervent Socialist enough not to care a tinker's curse for her title or for her acknowledged position as favorite of His Royal Highness Edward, Prince of Wales. He, probably more than any man the petted beauty had as yet come up against, got the true measure of her, seeing clean and clear right through her social snobbery and posing.

"She was very angry," he records. "She argued

that buying all the things necessary for her ball was good for trade. I then got round to talking about Socialism. Three times she asked me, with supercilious politeness, if I really believed in it."

At last he lost patience and suddenly rounded on her.

"Lady Warwick! You have asked me three times if I am a hypocrite. It may seem strange and new to you, but I am not."

She gulped. Then, recovering herself, she stood up. "Mr. Blatchford," she said icily, "I am not used to being spoken to like that."

She later declared that she came out of that office converted to the blinding truths of Socialist justice. That is not true, of course. She rarely told the truth, and she had the habit of dramatizing any event in her life. She did, however, tell Blatchford some time afterward that she went from Fleet Street to Paddington and sat on a platform seat there, thinking about what he had said and studying his Socialist arguments. She was also, of course, waiting for her train, the first-class carriage, the drive to Warwick Castle and dinner off gold plate.

But it is true that she did become a Socialist. At least, she declared herself as such, and in all fairness one must admit that even if her conversion was not basically sincere or even fundamentally reasoned out, the fact that she lent her name and her title and her social eminence to the Socialist Party may have made many folks realize that, after all, the Socialist folk could not be all cloth-capped and dangerous revolutionaries.

It can be argued that hers was a kind of idealistic William Morris Socialism—in 1912 she actually published a book, *William Morris: His Home and Haunts*. Nevertheless, she was undoubtedly a valuable capture for the Socialist Party. The speeches she made during her political campaigning read well today. Her demands for school meals, for the nationalization of land and for technical education equal to that being given in the United States and in Switzerland were all good Socialism. Undoubtedly such speeches were buttressed with facts and opinions provided by her Socialist friends, but because of who she was they reached an audience that probably would not have deigned to listen to rank-and-file Socialist workers. Also, in the 1906 and 1910 elections she characteristically injected drama and color into political canvassing by such actions as driving voters to the polls in a little red car.

She went the whole hog. She sent her own children to the local elementary school, and although she had always loved hunting—she had always looked a pretty fetching figure in stock and bowler—she even turned against this sport, judging it an idle and expensive caper for a Socialist woman to indulge in when so many poor people had less money for their daily bread than the cost of a hunter's daily oats. It is probably uncharitable to suspect that the unpaid bills now beginning to pile up in her desk, including bills for fodder and stable appurtenances, may have influenced her somewhat in this renunciation of an aristocratic sport.

Now that we know so many of the secrets of poor Daisy, it seems strange to read what was written about her in later years—to read, for instance, the Socialist newspaper, the *Daily Herald*, recording: "In Socialism she found an object for all the energy, all the fine enthusiasm, and generous kindness, which made up her nature."

Let us be kind. There is some truth buried in that eulogy. She had energy: anyone who could take on marriage and Lord Charles Beresford and the Prince of Wales into the bargain and also pursue the frantic social round demanded of a lady of society in those days must have had abundant energy, and it was not her fault that from an early age she had been schooled to burn up that energy in foolish and amoral channels. She had enthusiasm, too: feverish enthusiasm that she could devote to ill-advised projects like her private zoo with its bishop-chasing emus at Warwick, or, for that matter, dreaming up and planning a ruinously expensive *bal poudré*. Generous kindness? She even had some of that. To her personal staff, to her tenants, to the poor at the gates of Warwick Castle she was generous and she was kind. If she had not been brought up by blindly

autocratic and buttressed aristocrats, had not been
singled out for Royal petting by that old dynasty-
creator Victoria, had married differently and been
taught to love honestly—if all these unlikely things
could have happened to the girl born as Frances
Maynard, then her impulsive warmth might have
made her more generous and more kind in a wider
sense and led to more than social alms-giving and
grande-dame relief of the immediate and obvious
distress at her castle doors.

She began a series of good works. The social
beauty who had once been Edward's "Daisy wife"
founded such proper establishments as a college at
Studley Castle in Warwickshire for the "training of
the daughters of professional men in horticulture,
dairy farming, bee and poultry keeping," a home for
seventeen crippled children in Warwick, and on the
Easton Lodge estate a science and technical school
for boys and girls from the rural districts of Essex.
She became renowned as "an assiduous worker for
the betterment of thwarted lives," and in her entry in
Who's Who she claimed to have established at Warwick Castle and Easton Lodge a "complete organisa-
tion for the welfare of the poor and the nursing of
the sick." In fact, the favorite of Edward, Prince of
Wales, eventually rose to the rank of President of
the Essex Needlework Guild.

Ideologically her Socialism was sometimes a bit
shaky, and occasionally the conditioning of her social

upbringing oozed through the cracks of her political image. As when on an American lecture tour, to the astonishment of an audience that had come to sit at the feet of a real English Countess who had become a Socialist, she poured scorn on the social pretensions of lowly born women and went on to explain the noble purpose of true aristocracy. Or when she wrote: "It may be noted that today there is scarcely a dividing line between women of various social classes in the cut and quality of their underwear."

Yet, although her conversion to Socialism may at first have been nothing more than a romantic and delightfully eccentric showing-off, the impact of that interview with Blatchford and her subsequent study of Socialist principles eventually implanted in her a certain consistency in her approach to politics. She demonstrated this, for instance, on the occasion when some Essex friends, obviously still seeing her merely as a generous *grande dame* who sympathized with the plight of the working class, asked her to subscribe to a presentation to some Essex railwaymen who had refused to strike with their work mates. Her refusal to give any support to "blacklegs" showed these petitioners how little they understood a Socialist.

However, being Frances Warwick, she could not fail to make a tragic drama out of her conversion. It had been, according to her, a great sacrifice. It had ruined her socially, cast her down from her great height as leading hostess in the social world

and the intimate beloved of Prince Edward. Blatchford claims that she told him that Edward had
threatened never to see her again, so furious was he
with her conversion to Left-wing politics.

Poor Frances. It is a pity to rob her of that
drama; almost cruel to this formerly beautiful and
sexually desirable woman to reveal the truth.

Actually, she and Edward were together on several occasions after she became officially a member
of the Socialist Party, and she even aired some of
her newly formed political views to him. They
were not, naturally, to his taste. In any case, this
dictator of society shared with a later dictator of a
grosser stamp the opinion that a woman's rightful
place was in the nursery, in the kitchen and—most
certainly—in bed. He did not think women should
be politicians. He listened to her Socialist arguments
with amused tolerance, and when she tried to tell
him why she had become a Socialist he yawned.

Yawned! That yawn is significant. That Edward,
Prince of Wales, might be reduced to yawning when
a woman tried to argue politics can be understood.
But that he could yawn about anything closely
connected with the life and activities of his "dear
Daisy wife" had, so far as Frances Warwick was
concerned, more sinister implications. The sad and
brutal truth is that Edward did not toss Frances
Warwick out of his life because she had been converted to Socialism. On the contrary, the fire of

revolutionary ardor in a lovely Countess could have
added a little piquancy to their association, and it is
quite certain that on that occasion years before when
she came, beautiful in her distress, to Marlborough
House to implore his protection against the Beresfords, he would have wanted to lure her to his bed
even if she had been wearing a red cap and carrying
an anarchist bomb. He would certainly not have
yawned.

But time was marching on. At least, Edward
thought so. He was now past his middle fifties, and to
him it must have seemed that his life had degenerated
into one long frustration of waiting. He was still a
comparatively unemployed Royal because that old
black-gowned widow his mother insisted on keeping
her plump hands on the seals and scepters and
dispatch boxes. He could still hope, of course, so long
as his doctors maintained him in moderate health, to
become King-Emperor, for even Victoria could not
live forever—though sometimes it looked damned
near like it. But his principal preoccupation was not
about his Royal future. What worried him was his
future as a *man*. That was much less secure. He had
reached what is inevitably a dismal age for any man
who has enjoyed the sensual pleasures of life with
such robust appetite. He began feeling his years. A
twinge of indigestion after too much ptarmigan pie;
a lack of appetite when he faced the piled-up delica-
cies at Chatsworth or Rules; a tired irritation when

he had to ride in robed and bemedaled pomp on those
state occasions Victoria delegated to her heir while
conserving her strength for the real Royal power of
her Palace desk and private arguments with Pre-
miers. To Edward such twinges and wearinesses and
failing appetites were bad enough, but there were
others that were even sadder. There seemed, when he
looked at the calendar, very few years left for the
enjoyment of the delights which lovely women can
provide. How very long ago it now seemed since the
night when Nellie Clifden had been smuggled to his
bed at the Curragh. Yes, it was a long time ago, yet
it was too early for any man to sink into a dull
routine of domesticity, as sometimes it seemed to him
that he was sinking with Daisy. After all, he was
only fifty-seven. Perhaps he needed, more than any
restoratives that doctors could pump into him, the
natural stimulus of young and lovely and exhila-
rating female companionship. In short, he felt that
perhaps he needed a change to revitalize him. He
began, delicately, to disengage himself from darling
Daisy.

Frances must have recognized the signs. By now
she knew Edward well and she had surely seen and
heard enough during her nearly nine years as his
favorite to know that her reign was coming to an end.
It says a lot for Edward—and it does indicate that
Frances had convinced the trusting Prince that her
affection was deep and lasting—that he did not

desert her completely. In public she salved her pride
by posing as a martyr to her political convictions,
claiming that her espousal of the faith of Socialism
had lost her Edward's love, but in private she kept in
touch with him. He did not forget the love he had felt
for her or the joys she had given him, and felt toward
her the fondness one feels toward any person who has
done one good and faithful service. Almost the same
kind of genial fondness that he had for his dear
patient Alexandra. In fact, as darling Daisy sub-
sided into his past she seemed in his mind to merge
with Alexandra, and he actually tried to formulate a
discreet plan to bring these two dear friends together
in amicable and mutually consoling harmony.

This happened at a time when Frances was beginning to feel the social draft. Her liaison with Edward
had naturally made her *persona non grata* at Court.
That had not mattered at all when she was Edward's
constant companion. The parties he took her to as his
"darling Daisy" were jollier by far than any formal
Court occasions. But now that he was no longer
taking her around she found herself socially ma-
rooned. The hostesses who invited him to country
houses could no longer invite her. The more formal
and more proper hostesses who enjoyed the honor of
Alexandra's company were, on the other hand, uncertain whether they dared invite the woman who
had been her husband's favorite.

At last, when Frances had finally accepted that there was no longer any hope of retaining Edward's love, she began an attempt to return to the social scene as an accepted and acceptable lady of title. The only way to do so was, of course, to be received again at Court. That could only be achieved by being received by Alexandra.

So in January 1898 she wrote to Edward the letter with which she planned to initiate her campaign to win social rehabilitation. The years had taught her a lot. This letter to her former lover was not a foolish emotional letter from a deserted woman, like the one she had sent to Lord Charles Beresford more than eight years earlier. This was a careful letter, exquisitely and delicately phrased. In it she was making the great renunciation, selflessly withdrawing herself from a noble and not unworthy love. It was full of affection, but affection of only a nostalgic character in which she looked back on the happy years they had spent together. This time the memories she evoked were memories not of passion but of interests and pleasures they had shared with dignity and grace. There was one difficult hurdle to surmount, and even this she managed with infinite tact, inserting with the utmost delicacy the statement that their friendship had now been platonic for some years.

She was, of course, not writing to Edward at all.

She was really writing, indirectly, to Alexandra. She had calculatingly planned the letter as the kind a man could show to his wife almost with pride—as Edward could show it to Alexandra—as proof of the noble and deep affection he was capable of arousing in such a wonderful woman.

Having gone so far, she took her courage in both hands and pushed her plan a bit more forward. She wrote also to Alexandra. In this letter she expressed the fear that perhaps "enemies" of hers might have poisoned the Princess' ears against her with unpleasant gossip. She was conscious now that some of her actions might have led the Princess to think badly of her, but she wanted the Princess at least to know that for her part she knew Edward's dear wife was a noble and gracious woman, too noble and gracious to bear malice for past errors.

The plan brilliantly succeeded. The letter reached Edward when he was staying with the Devonshires at Chatsworth. His wife was with him there—as Frances well knew from reading the list of guests in *The Times*. The letter went straight to Edward's ingenuous heart. Immediately he showed it to Alexandra and then wrote back to Frances.

His generous impulsive letter was that very same one which sixteen years later Lady Warwick showed to Arthur du Cros in her Eaton Square drawing room when she told him she hoped to earn more than £100,000 from her Royal lover's correspondence, the

one of which the Tory M.P. read only the opening
lines before turning in shocked surprise to the signature.

> *My own lovely little Daisy,*
>
> *It is difficult for me to describe how touched I
> was by your beautiful letter which reached me
> this morning which crossed mine from San-
> dringham which will have reached you today.*
>
> *I gave it to the Princess to read. She was
> moved to tears, and said she felt very sorry for
> you and that "out of evil good would come."*
>
> *She kept the letter to read it again and
> return it to me at tea-time, and begged me to
> thank you for the letter she received from you
> this morning, which she showed me. She begged
> me to tell you that you had no enemies that she
> was aware of who were friends of hers and that
> your name was not mentioned to her—or by her.*

Edward then gave Frances the good news that she
wanted, assuring her that Alexandra would receive
her.

> *I know, my Darling, that she will now meet
> you with pleasure, so that your position is,
> thank God! better now than it ever was since we
> have been such friends, and I do not despair, in
> time, that you and she may become quite good
> friends.*

He must have thought everything was working out beautifully. Frances had accepted her demotion without reproaches, and now he could assure her that with Alexandra's recognition Frances was actually in a better position socially than she had been even when she was his reigning favorite. So he began speculating on some way in which he might bring the two of them together without making too much social fuss about it. They might, for instance, meet as fellow workers in some charitable enterprise.

We must also endeavour to get up some object in common—some philanthropic one I mean—which may have a common interest to both. It is so inexpressibly sad and unfortunate that we are unable to meet now, as in a short time so much might be discussed and settled "viva voce" which cannot be done by letter.

She really quite forgives and condones the past, as I have corroborated what you wrote about our friendship having been platonic for some years. You could not help, my loved one, writing to me as you did—though it gave me a pang—after the letters I have received from you for nearly nine years! But I think I could read "between the lines" everything you wished to convey.

The end of your beautiful letter touched me more than anything—but how could you, my loved one, for a moment imagine that I should withdraw my friendship from you? On the contrary I mean to befriend you more than ever, and you cannot prevent my giving you the same love as the friendship I have always felt for you.

Certainly the Princess has been an angel of goodness throughout all this, but then she is a Lady, and never could do anything that was mean or small.

Though our interests, as you have often said, lie apart, still we have that sentimental feeling of affinity which cannot be eradicated by time— and we must still have so many objects in common.

Long may that remain so!

You do not tell me how you are, my poor little love? but are I hope better, and trust that by complete rest and quiet your health may not suffer and that all will go well with you till the proper time.

A kind and warm and generous letter indeed, but at the same time a letter which delicately underlines how distant they now were from each other. Yet Edward was still anxious to assure his darling Daisy that her social position was safe and that she still had his trust, and three days later he was writing to her again, this time in reply to a worried letter in which she had expressed fears that perhaps her letters to him were being opened by others. He set her mind at rest.

Your dear little note reached me this morning. I can assure you that all letters directed by yourself in your own dear handwriting have always reached me safely, and no danger of being opened, but naturally I can understand, my Darling, that you have every reason to feel nervous, though I can assure you that your position is better than it ever has been, and it is so essential that the world should have the opportunity of seeing that there is no desire of your being shunned in any way.

In that letter he still addressed her as "My own lovely little Daisy," still signed himself "Your only love." But those forms of address were now merely habit. Suddenly, he must have realized, he was free. Frances herself had indicated the way in which he could repay her for the pleasures she had provided. He could now perform the final service to "darling Daisy," steer her to an honorable place in society beside his dear wife, Alexandra. And then?

Things could hardly have happened more quickly. Only seven weeks after writing that letter to his "Daisy wife" he went to dinner at the London home of the Hon. George Keppel, a brother of the Earl of Albemarle, an aide-de-camp to Queen Victoria.

That dinner party was a crucial one in Edward's life and in Daisy's career.

It was the result of an encounter a few days earlier when, at Sandown Races, Edward had met Alice Keppel, the woman who became almost overnight the last love of his life. Many years later an aunt of Winston Churchill, Mrs. Jack Leslie, claimed that her husband was responsible for bringing the two together. Jack Leslie, she said, was strolling in the paddock with the young and beautiful Mrs. George Keppel when he met Edward and presented her. Edward was immediately taken with her and, almost before the introductions ceased, asked her to accompany him. She accepted the Royal invitation. Leaving Jack Leslie alone, the two went off, already chatting amicably. According to Mrs. Leslie, the smile on the Prince's face indicated to her husband that he had little chance of seeing Alice Keppel for the rest of that day.

Thus, suddenly, began Edward's last liaison. It endured through all his reign, right up to his death on May 6, 1910, in his sixty-ninth year. In fact, he dined with her in Grosvenor Street just before his last illness. She thought he looked ill and persuaded him to go home early, and a few evenings later, when it was certain that he was dying, the sad and forgiving Alexandra sent a message asking Alice Keppel to join her at his bedside at Buckingham Palace.

Alice Keppel was good-looking, vivacious, clever and, as she proved throughout the twelve years she was Edward's favorite, discreet. When they first met, she was twenty-nine. A nice age, the fifty-six-year-old Prince must have thought. Eight years younger, in fact, than dear darling discarded Daisy.

It is recorded that Edward made a point of never speaking in Alice Keppel's presence the name of her predecessor, Frances Warwick. It is pretty certain that neither would he ever breathe the name of Alice Keppel in Frances Warwick's presence. Not that he was nowadays very much in her presence. He saw Frances increasingly at big social functions, at the theatre and the opera, at garden parties. He smiled and bowed. She curtsied and passed on, the beautiful Countess of Warwick, the Socialist noblewoman, the doer of good works and champion of the poor, the "assiduous worker for the betterment of thwarted lives." With Alexandra so compliant and forgiving, there was no fear of Frances Warwick not being accepted back into society, and amid the new gossip about the vivacious Alice Keppel the old whispers about "darling Daisy" died painlessly away. But the pleasure Frances Warwick found in her new role as *grande dame* and politician was clouded with worries. Already she was beginning to glimpse on the horizon clouds more difficult to disperse than the transitory shadows of social disapproval. The gross extravagance that had already swallowed up her own fortune was now making deep inroads into the coffers of the Warwick estate.

Ursula Bloom, in recalling stories her father told about Frances, says: "Lady Warwick never had a clue about money. She took it for granted that everyone was rich, and spent like water. She amused herself by giving enormous parties, often not knowing many of the people who appeared, for the age of the gate-crasher is no new venture."

Her income from the estates and also her capital were being lapped up, not only by parties and *bals poudrés*, but also by other extravagant conceits of which the flow of creations from the House of Worth and jewelers' bills for the resetting of gems were one item and the private zoo she had tried to create at Warwick Castle was another. The zoo, incidentally, was not only a costly enterprise, it was also a dangerous and on one occasion a fatal one. We have mentioned the spectacle, described by Harvey Bloom, of two emus chasing a bishop through the shrubberies. There was a more tragic occurrence when the pretty wild deer Frances allowed to roam in the courtyard killed their keeper, and she herself was disappointed and hurt when the dear little baby elephant she had bought at the door grew up into such a big creature with an outrageously expensive appetite.

But her most expensive pet had undoubtedly been Edward, Prince of Wales. It was of course not the whole truth, but there was some truth in the claim she made—when she tried to justify her disgraceful plan of selling Edward's love letters—that her financial ruin had been caused by the vast expense of entertaining Edward and his friends. After all, he had ruined other people that way. His boon companion Christopher Sykes, for instance.

This gravely bearded and dignified gentleman is one of the most pitiably tragic figures of the Edwardian era. So servilely devoted was he to his Prince that he allowed Edward to use him, in moments of perversely vulgar ruffianism, as a butt for messy practical jokes. A revolting scene at the Marlborough Club, the club Edward founded and of which Sykes was a foundation member, illustrates shockingly the depths to which an intelligent and dignified man like Sykes can sink when he surrenders a man's birthright of pride and independence for snobbish attendance on a capricious vulgarian. On that occasion Edward, in an outburst of contemptuous and almost Tudor arrogance, humiliated "the Great Xtopher" by emptying a glass of brandy over his head. Sykes, with besotted loyalty, submitted without protest or movement, letting the spirit flow over his face and trickle from his beard. The words he uttered—the formula of a craven and submissive courtier—brought a howl of laughter from the assembled guests: "As Your Royal Highness pleases." The phrase passed into history as a ludicrous joke.

He endured this kind of insult for years, all the time he was plunging himself into bankruptcy in the lavish entertainment he mounted for Edward's enjoyment. There is, perhaps, a little poetic justice in the fact that it was when Sykes could no longer afford to entertain his Prince at his Yorkshire home for the Doncaster races that Edward went instead to Tranby Croft for the weekend and suffered for it. When finally Sykes did shudder into the final disgrace of bankruptcy, Edward was moved to say remorsefully, "What a thoroughly bad business." But he would have done nothing more than utter words of regret had not Christopher's virago of a sister-in-law forced her way into his presence in London and, by some powerful threat as yet undisclosed, forced the potentate to help in paying some of the debts.

There was Lord Hardwicke, too, the Earl who added to the luster of the Edwardian era by inventing the polished silk hat. In entertaining Edward and his friends and keeping up with the demands of the Marlborough House crowd, he, too, lost the main part of his fortune, as well as his ancestral home. So one must accept Frances Warwick's statement that her affair with Edward had been a vastly expensive business.

The years passed. The debts at Warwick and Easton grew. She kept her brave Socialist face to the world. She spoke courageously at political meetings, she spent generously on her welfare work, she entertained regularly—though her guests were now mostly Socialists. Easton Lodge was open house for Labour candidates and trade-union leaders as well as secretaries of local Labour parties and world-renowned "Red revolutionaries." But the creditors were closing in. At last came the humiliations that precede the final collapse: the need to borrow money, the attempt "to buy time," the snubs of being refused goods at local stores and the approach of bankruptcy.

In the summer of 1914 she found herself scraping the bottom of an empty barrel in search of a few pounds. On that day when she drove back from Leamington, quivering with fury at having suffered humiliation at the hands of a shopkeeper, the words of the Warwick coat-of-arms, *Vix ea nostro voco,* must have seemed a sour mockery to the onetime Royal favorite as she walked through the debt-burdened and mortgaged grandeur of the ancestral home. "I scarcely call these things our own"—never had any motto seemed more true than that. There were treasures enough around her, lots of things worth a lot of money, and, as always in times of national uncertainty and political unrest, the prices of art treasures were bouncing up in the sale rooms. There were the Rubenses, the Van Dycks, the Holbeins and the Lelys, for instance. There were other priceless pieces—that "Warwick Vase" and that clock of Marie Antoinette's, constant reminder of the sumptuous *bal poudré* she had staged in the state rooms in the days of her grandeur. But even had it been possible to sell these family treasures, even if they had not been protected by the laws of inheritance or clamped in position by the weight of mortgages, one could never think of parting with them. To strip Warwick walls of such costly beauties would be as bad as to stop being dressed by Worth. Nor at Easton, where devoted family servants, only half aware that their wages might not be paid, dutifully polished the gold plate, could Frances, Countess of Warwick, contemplate divesting herself of the merest scrap of her social opulence merely to satisfy a few insolent tradesmen or pay back loans to moneylending Jews and millionaire creditors like Arthur du Cros.

Yet there was something that could be sold without robbing her homes of a single glittering treasure. She could sell herself. Not her present self, of course —not that aging remnant of a beauty which, now merely a legend, was still automatically ascribed to her whenever her name reached print. The Frances Warwick she could sell was the Frances Warwick of the past. Stowed away in her desk was a bundle of letters which would make certain that she would profit hugely from the sale.

It was at this dire period that she must have recalled something said to her years before, perhaps at a supper party after the theatre. Was it at Kettners, or Rules, or at the Café Royal? She could not remember where, but vividly she could remember a hairy vulgar little man with a booming voice and a bold manner she had first met in Edward's company at a luncheon party given by Lady Dorothy Nevill. At this later meeting with him, when she was no longer Edward's special favorite, the journalist, taking advantage of her fallen state, had had the temerity to insinuate that the stories she could tell about her Royal lover could be worth a fortune. The name? Frank Harris. She must occasionally have seen the odious little journal he had published or edited, *Modern Society.* It no longer appeared. It had apparently been swallowed up in bankruptcy. So, she probably argued, Harris was perhaps as much in need of money as she was, and might be prepared to work for her. At least the idea must have struck her as worth investigating. She could find out what he would say. He might know whether the letters were worth as much as she hoped.

Was it really a nice and proper thing to sell a lover's letters and the secrets of her bed? That question would not intrude deeply into Frances Warwick's calculations. To the Frances Warwicks of this world the inability to pay the dressmaker is greater shame than the loss of honor. After all, "dear Edward" had been dead for four years. His son King George must surely know—or if he did not, then the fact must be made plain to him—that it was really his father who had reduced "darling Daisy" to her present plight. "Dear Edward" might, in fact, be happy to know that four years after his death he still had the power to comfort his "own sweet wife."

The evidence in the "Darling Daisy" dossier suggests that she first got into touch with Harris through the agency of some never named "trusted friend," and it seems obvious that Harris' reaction was even more enthusiastic than she had hoped for. He was convinced that the story of her life—including, of course, every word King Edward had written to her—would still be as valuable as when he had proposed the idea years ago. Harris, however, would not fail to impress upon her that the writing of such a story demanded the application of professional skill. Only a brilliant author could mold it into the glorious shape it deserved. Someone like Frank Harris? Well, he was burdened at the moment with important creative projects, as, naturally, any writer of his eminence always was. Yet he had such warm memories of the charming and beautiful Countess of Warwick that he would be happy to step down from Parnassus and help her. He could assist her in assembling the raw material of her past—any diaries or records and letters. He could even help her to write the book. That was, of course, dependent upon whether the material she mentioned was as good as he hoped it was. King Edward's letters, for

instance? It was possible that a man in such a
position might have been too discreet to write to her
the kind of letters the public would want to read.
Perhaps, he feared, they were only guarded formal
communications. He would like to see them to assess
their potential worth. Would she please send them to
him?

She didn't send them. She knew enough—or
guessed enough—about Frank Harris not to do
anything so foolish: knew more about him, in fact,
than she had disclosed in her first apparently impulsive approach. She would take care to let Frank
Harris think that he had a trusting and ingenuous
woman on his hands.

She did not think it wise to send such valuable
documents through the post, but a friend would
come to Paris and show them to Harris.

When he did see the letters his reaction was
impressive. He was now wildly eager to see the book
written and published. In fact, he reported, he had
already taken the liberty of discussing the project
confidentially with the Paris representatives of an
American publishing house. The publishers were
vastly interested and wanted him to go to America to
make a deal. He was confident that they would pay,
at the very least, £100,000.

Harris, of course, would certainly insist that the
deal would have to be made through him. It was his
standing as a writer and their knowledge of his

abilities that made the publishers so confident of the book's potential value. Yet he obviously assured Frances that, despite the fact that he was much sought after as a writer and consequently could demand the highest fees from publishers who were on their knees begging for his work, his services would not cost her a penny. So convinced was he that the book would be an enormous financial success that he would be content to do the work on the expectation of a percentage of the royalties. Apparently he told her that they could, however, discuss such unimportant financial details when he had the joy of seeing her again, and hoped that would be soon. It seems that he asked if there was any chance of her being in Paris in the near future. He must have expressed his regret that he could not come over to London at the moment, and probably pleaded pressure of work, not wanting to tell her the real reason why it would be inconvenient to show his debtor face in London just then.

She agreed to meet him in Paris on July 7. That promise was made to keep Harris nicely "on the boil." She would now be feeling happier and more confident than she had felt for months. Things were indeed going very well. She had the assurance of a clever, even if unscrupulous, journalist that if the worst came to the worst and she was forced to publish "dear Edward's" letters, they would earn her at least £100,000. A nice round figure. Enough, she obviously felt, to hoist her clean out of the mire of debt.

But, of course, the worst need not come to the worst. Frances Warwick would certainly be aware that the mere *threat* of publishing the letters could earn her as much as actually publishing them. Frank Harris had been useful as a "valuer" and given her a working idea of the market price for her treasure. She could use his valuation and his obvious eagerness to edit her memoirs as a lever to prise open the coffers of people who would be more anxious to keep the letters out of print than see them on the bookstalls. For her own part, she certainly knew it would be altogether more comfortable for her if the letters were not published. Publication would, as she told Arthur du Cros, blast her reputation. She did not relish the thought of being a social outcast.

So, when she had fixed a meeting with Harris, it was time for the next move. She decided to write to Arthur du Cros. After all, he was a creditor of hers, so would naturally be interested in the efforts she was making to pay her debts. He was also a distinguished Tory M.P. and would undoubtedly have access to personages sufficiently sensitive to the necessity for silence about Royal scandals and sufficiently wealthy to pay for such silence. She remembered the efforts Lord Salisbury had made to keep the Beresford affair out of print. To her the circumstances of 1914 must have seemed very much the same. The Prime

Minister, Mr. Asquith, although a radical with an anti-aristocracy Chancellor, Mr. Lloyd George, in his ranks, would be equally anxious to protect the dignity and honor of the Royal House, particularly in view of the fact that while Britain was facing the threat of civil war in Ireland King George was being savagely and uncharitably criticized for his good-natured interference in political affairs.

"Blackmail" is an ugly word, and particularly ugly when used in association with an aristocrat and the president of the Essex Needlework Guild. But it is a word difficult to avoid in telling the story of Frances Warwick's £100,000 intrigue. It is impossible to believe what she told Arthur du Cros: that she was prepared to destroy her name in society by publishing the story of her love affair with Edward. So many of the things she said and did later, delaying the publication, haggling and threatening, are utterly inconsistent with her avowed resolve to publish and be damned. Only when we accept the repellent fact that a woman of noble birth and public eminence can stoop to extorting money by blackmail do we see that all her utterances and actions click neatly into place, each one understandable, each one consistent with a scheme designed to sell *not* her memoirs but her silence. Consider, for instance, her action in giving that Beresford letter to Arthur du Cros on the pretext that she was allowing him the opportunity of authenticating the

handwriting. If, as she had said, she had been working for many months on her memoirs and they were
now completed, what possible reason was there for
anyone, and why Arthur du Cros in any case, to
authenticate the handwriting? Even apart from this
question of handwriting, why give Arthur du Cros
the letter at all? She could explain away having
invited him to Eaton Square and telling him about
her project by arguing that it had become necessary
to assure a creditor that very soon she would be
solvent. But if the book was now ready for the
publishers and Harris was awaiting her in Paris
before going to America to finalize the deal, what
earthly reason was there for letting Arthur du Cros
hurry off from Eaton Square with the letter?

There is no other explanation than that she had
selected Arthur du Cros as an intermediary in an
extortion plot. She knew him as an influential Tory
of the truest blue, one of those men who possessed
something which even in 1914 was in some quarters
considered a shade old-fashioned: the attribute of
blind patriotic belief in the tradition and dignity and
glory of King and Country. In choosing him she had
nicely calculated that he would be the very man to be
deeply shocked at the thought of a Royal scandal
being uncovered, and a man who—quite apart from
any political and social ambitions he might have—
would enjoy feeling himself a knight errant loyally
serving his Royal Family if he could be instrumental

in covering up an unfortunate secret in its past. It is obvious that Frances Warwick did not choose Arthur du Cros, as she claimed, to advise her in her crisis, but chose him really as an ideal postman to carry news of her project to Royal ears. She almost certainly chose with equal care the letter he would carry.

My analysis of Frances Warwick's money-raising operation and my accusation that her methods were tortuously and calculatedly dishonest might seem uncharitable—might, indeed, be criticized as mere supposition based upon insubstantial evidence. But the indictment is securely founded, for there exists, available for anyone to read, a statement Frances Warwick herself made many years later. This statement can be accepted as an admission that in 1914 she was using du Cros as an intermediary, an ingenuous and unsuspecting one, in a double game of extortion.

The statement appeared in 1929, fifteen years after that June afternoon when she was making du Cros believe that she intended to sell her secrets and "dear Edward's" letters for £100,000. It appears in *Life's Ebb and Flow*, the book Frances Warwick published when she at last got round to writing her memoirs. Her book is quite a period piece, a quite readable account of the kind of life led by any wealthy and aristocratic woman in that lush and vulgar period of England's history. But the perceptive reader of this outpouring of social anecdote and titled chit-chat can almost smell that crucial moment when the great revelation ought to come, the moment when the glamorous story of her affair with Edward and his letters should explode on the page. Instead, at this point there is a quite obvious lurch in the narrative, a sudden intake of breath, a pregnant pause. Instead of Edward rolling in with his "Darling Daisy" letters, we are treated to a high-minded homily from the noble author. With restrained passion and an attitude of injured pride she refers to fears that had been entertained for a long time by people in society and in government—fears that she would publish certain important letters. Such fears, she assures us, were utterly groundless. How could anyone believe that any noblewoman could ever be guilty of such a despicable breach of trust? That was something that was just not done.

Is she in 1929 speaking the truth? If so, she was lying in 1914. Or vice versa. She cannot have it both ways.

There we have it. In 1929 she says that anyone who believed she could dream of publishing "dear Edward's" letters was foolish. But, as we now know, it was something which, in 1914, Arthur du Cros, Frank Harris, the Royal Family and, eventually, a High Court Judge were foolish enough to believe. She gave them every reason for believing it. Among the papers discovered in Switzerland are letters of hers and other documents revealing clearly how she went about it.

The first revealing letter of hers is the one which she wrote to Arthur du Cros on June 24, 1914. What a coincidence that it should be written on that day of all days. It is almost certain that on a table beside her on that day would stand a vase with a great wealth of red roses bought at the door of Easton Lodge that morning from a charity collector. For it was Alexandra Rose Day. On that very morning the revered widow of that same "dear Edward" who had been Frances Warwick's lover would be riding out of Marlborough House, bowing her head to folks waving roses and cheering the beloved Queen Mother. Along The Mall to the gates of Buckingham Palace, where she was going to lunch with her son King George and Queen Mary, were some of the twenty thousand rose-sellers who were collecting for charities in London on Alexandra Day.

The letter, written, as I have described, in bold easy-flowing script, has all the appearance of being penned freely and impulsively; but, knowing Frances Warwick, one wonders how many drafts she may have made, studying just where to plant the threatening pregnant phrases to alert du Cros to the urgency of the communication. Then, having drafted it to her liking, she could copy it out quickly and easily and make it look ingenuously forthright.

The letter did what she wanted. It brought du

Cros to that interview in her Eaton Square drawing room in which she tactfully and delicately steered him into becoming her tool, a collaborator in her plot, and then sent him on his way with the Beresford letter, the one letter best suited for the opening of her attack, the letter which would bring the memory of "darling Daisy" vividly back to the minds of King George and his courtiers, reminding them disquietingly of the past Edward scandal when even the formidably entrenched potentate Victoria had been moved to say "the Monarchy almost is in danger." Knowing what we do now, we can well imagine the alarm aroused at St. James's and Buckingham Palace when, five days later, Arthur du Cros placed this letter in the hands of a faithful Royal servant, the Earl of Albemarle, and told him of Frances Warwick's plan "to tell all."

4

ALARM AT THE PALACE

Arthur du Cros was determined that King George should be told immediately about Lady Warwick's threat to publish Edward's letters. Even before he left Eaton Square he had made up his mind that this was the proper course, but his later discovery of the startling implications of the Beresford letter made him feel that no time must be lost in warning King George.

He did not realize that this was exactly what Frances Warwick hoped would happen. He was still seeing her in the role she had acted before him: a woman so plagued with debt that she was hardly aware that the publication of the letters could do incalculable harm not only to the Royal Family but also to the nation. Even yet Arthur du Cros did not realize that actually he had been drawn into a plot to extort money from the Royal Family.

It was natural that du Cros, a patriotic and also ambitious politician, should welcome an opportunity of showing himself a loyal liege of his sovereign. So much so that he would really have liked to take the letter and news of Lady Warwick's threat to King George in person. But he could not do that, of course. Even a millionaire Tory M.P. could not go to Buckingham Palace, ask to see the King and say, "Your Majesty, here is one of your father's love letters. The woman in the case intends to publish it and others in America. What are you going to do about it?"

In any case, the King was out of town, on a state visit to the mining areas of the Midlands, and staying with the Duke of Portland at Welbeck Abbey. So Arthur du Cros must let the King have the news through the "accepted channels" of the Palace. He must hand the information to someone close to the King—the closer the better. Fortunately, he knew personally a man well suited for this delicate operation. The Earl of Albemarle, an aide-de-camp to King George, was a fellow member of the Carlton Club, and Arthur du Cros had met him on a sufficient number of social occasions to consider him among his friends. Albemarle, du Cros decided, would be an ideal man to approach. His brother, the Hon. Derek

Keppel, was Master of the Royal Household. Another brother, George, was the husband of that same lovely Mrs. George Keppel who had succeeded Frances Warwick as Edward's favorite. Even more apposite, Albemarle had also been an aide-de-camp to King Edward and would therefore certainly appreciate the full significance of the Beresford letter and the dangerous situation caused by Lady Warwick's threats.

Du Cros realized well enough that it was an unfortunate time to go anywhere near the Palace or the government on such an unpleasant errand. There was bad news enough. The political scene was darkened by the shadow of possible national disaster. There was the imminent threat of civil war in Ireland, a prospect so terrifying that even the daily recurring bombs and violence of the "Suffragettes" —those misguided women who were agitating for the right of women to vote—had faded to a mere nuisance. No one, of course, had as yet the slightest inkling that within five short weeks the whole of Europe would be shuddering into the vast tragedy of the Great War.

The *Times* which du Cros read at breakfast at his Edgware home, Canons, on the morning after his interview with Frances Warwick reported happily on King George's warm reception by cheering miners in the Midlands. There was also news of other Royal personages. At Kiel, where the British Navy was paying a courtesy visit, the Kaiser had proudly hoisted his own flag as a titular British admiral. And the Archduke Franz Ferdinand, heir to the Austro-Hungarian throne of the Emperor Franz Joseph, had arrived to attend army maneuvers near a Balkan town called Sarajevo. But reports from Ireland were gloomy and forbidding, and it was evident that within days the government, and perhaps the King, would have their hands full in dealing with a crisis of the first magnitude. Even so, du Cros argued—and argued rightly—the Lady Warwick affair could not be ignored. In fact, the delicate and dangerous political situation made it even more imperative that the threat of odious Royal scandal should be rapidly dispersed.

At his Regent Street office that morning du Cros discovered that Albemarle was out of town, staying at Queen Anne's Mead, the Windsor home of the Dowager Countess of Arran, former lady-in-waiting of King Edward's daughter Maud. The matter, du Cros judged, was too delicate to discuss on the telephone, so he decided to write to the Earl. It was a guarded letter.

> *My dear Lord Albemarle,*
>
> *Certain circumstances have quite acciden-
> tally come to my knowledge with regard to
> which I would like to consult you and ask your
> advice. I am leaving for Paris this afternoon,*

*but shall be in town again on Monday next, and
every day next week.*

*If you could spare me a few minutes at any
place convenient to yourself, I should be much
obliged.*

The trip to Paris had, apparently, no connection
with Frances Warwick's intention to meet Harris
there. Du Cros' diary of the Lady Warwick negotiations makes no mention of that weekend trip, and his
later detailed account of his conference with Harris
in Paris the following month makes it plain that that
conference was his first meeting with Harris for
many years. However, knowing du Cros' painstaking
methods, one can assume that if he did go to Paris
that weekend he would almost certainly make some
inquiries as to what Frank Harris was doing in that
city and what was now his standing there.

Du Cros' vague communication reached Albemarle
at Windsor on Saturday morning. What the courtier
thought about it we do not know. But we can hazard
a guess. Uppermost in all people's minds at the
moment was the trouble in Ireland. So, as du Cros
was Irish-born, founder in Dublin of a now vast
international industry, and a Tory M.P., Albemarle
would almost undoubtedly think that those "certain
circumstances" mentioned in du Cros' letter might
be some information the M.P. had unearthed through
contacts in Ireland. In the eyes of a courtier like

Albemarle, the Tory M.P. must have seemed a quite creditable person. After all, he was the descendant of a noble Huguenot family that had settled in Dublin in 1702, and Arthur du Cros was already a noted back-bencher who had convincingly demonstrated his imaginative foresight and confidence in modern inventions by persuading the government in 1909 to include "funds for aeronautics" in the Naval and Army estimates. Arthur du Cros can, in fact, be considered the Parliamentary godfather of the Flying Corps, which was to earn its wings in the 1914–18 war and eventually become the Royal Air Force. He had also contributed £6,000 toward the building of Britain's first airship.

But Albemarle, like most informed people in London at that time, would also be familiar with the romantic story of du Cros' rise to fame and fortune. In his youth Arthur du Cros had been an ardent racing cyclist, and this sport had actually been the root cause of his now considerable wealth. In May 1889, when he was eighteen, he was racing at Queen's College Sports and saw Hume, a well-known cyclist, win all the events on a bicycle equipped with a strange new device. Around the rim of each bicycle wheel was fixed a rubber tube covered with stout linen tape. The tube could be inflated by using the pump normally used for blowing up footballs. The man who had concocted the device was a Scotsman, John Boyd Dunlop, then a veterinary surgeon in Belfast. Du Cros asked to borrow the machine and four months later raced it at Ballsbridge, Dublin. Du Cros described the device as a "pneumatic tire," though spectators rudely called it a "pudding tire" and the race officials were doubtful whether cycle-racing ethics could allow the use of such a novelty. However, deciding to humor the youth's eccentricity, they allowed him to compete. Arthur won the race and the first prize.

He had won more. He had learned the immense potentialities the pneumatic tire could have—not only on such modest appliances as bicycles, but also for the new vehicle, the motor car, which at that time, under the impetus of such men as Daimler and Panhard, was at last being considered a commercial proposition.

John Boyd Dunlop had neither the capital nor, it seems, the commercial ambition to do much to develop his invention, but Arthur du Cros and his father, William Harvey du Cros, had both. They began manufacturing the tires at a Dublin factory, and within seven years the twenty-five-year-old racing cyclist was managing director of a £3,000,000 company, had laid the foundations of the family fortune and also of that giant Dunlop Rubber Company which within a few more years was a formidable worldwide industrial concern.

Indeed, the only thing about du Cros that might conceivably cause Albemarle any disquiet was that the Irish-born M.P. was reputed to be now a millionaire. Albemarle had had his fill of millionaires during his service as aide-de-camp to King Edward. The late King's love of their free-spending company and his unrestrained pleasure when enjoying their always lavish and sometimes improper hospitality had often offended the aristocratic sensibilities of Albemarle and other courtiers. However, Albermarle had to take cognizance of any communication from an influential Member of Parliament and would feel it his duty as a courtier to grant du Cros the interview he requested. If du Cros had some information from Ireland, it might be very useful indeed, because at that very moment the King and his advisers were trying to decide how far the Crown dare go—constitutionally and without offending the Commons—in an attempt to intervene in the Irish affair and avert national disaster.

But it was now the weekend. However urgent du Cros' information might be, nothing could be allowed to disturb the idyllic lull which even in times of crisis descends over Britain at the weekend. Nothing could be done until Monday in any case. Parliament had packed up its noisy arguments until then; M.P.'s and officers of state, like Albemarle and scores of other Londoners, were relaxing in the country. In fact, the only person working that weekend seemed to be King George himself. He had returned to Buck-

ingham Palace after opening new docks at Hull, and
on Saturday afternoon he reviewed the London Fire
Brigade in Hyde Park. As he drove to the park from
Buckingham Palace some Suffragettes threw a bunch
of pamphlets into his carriage. The next Royal
function in London was to be a state ball, the last of
the season, at Buckingham Palace on Monday evening.

Yet, after all, the tranquillity of that weekend was
suddenly shattered, and Albemarle had to return
hurriedly to London on Sunday. The Archduke
Franz Ferdinand had been assassinated in Sarajevo.
As he was an important Prince, heir to a great
empire, and had recently been a visitor to Buckingham Palace, Royal etiquette—as well as foreign
policy—demanded that some notice should be taken
of the upsetting event. During Sunday the King
agreed that the Court should go into mourning for a
week, and that he himself would pay formal regrets
at the Austro-Hungarian Embassy in Belgravia on
Monday. Some member of the Royal Family should,
he also agreed, be delegated to attend the funeral
which would, everyone believed on that June Sunday,
be the sad but final act of a Balkan tragedy. Because
of the mourning the state ball would have to be
canceled and an announcement to that effect circulated to the newspapers so that the ladies who had
already been trying on their new gowns for days and

the lords who had been polishing their medals and
orders would know in good time that the function was
off.

It was not until Monday that Lord Albemarle
found himself free to turn to Mr. Arthur du Cros'
request for an interview. By one of those little
coincidences that enliven history, there was published
in *The Times* on that Monday morning a "letter to
the editor" which, written by a distinguished Irish-
man, warned Britain of impending disaster. "We are
on the eve of an appalling catastrophe, towards
which we have been drifting for over two years. . . .
None of the proposals put forward to avoid civil war
can now be effective." The writer of the letter was
Lord Charles Beresford, former lover of Lady Warwick and now M.P. for Portsmouth.

Albemarle arranged to meet du Cros at their club,
the Carlton, on Tuesday morning. Du Cros took to
that interview two letters: Edward's Beresford letter
to his darling Daisy and Lady Warwick's letter to
du Cros in which she told him of her "secret work"
that would "blast" the reputation of herself and
others. The interview was conducted in a quiet corner
of the club's library.

Arthur du Cros opened the conversation by saying he needed Lord Albemarle's advice, the advice of
a friend, on a confidential and delicate matter. When
Albemarle indicated that he would, naturally, give
any advice possible, du Cros explained that the

matter concerned the Countess of Warwick.

It would be at this moment that Albemarle realized that du Cros' interview had nothing to do with Ireland or with politics, and when the M.P. drew from his frock coat a foolscap envelope, Albemarle would already be beginning to feel worried about what du Cros was leading up to.

Du Cros continued his explanation. He told Albemarle that he had met Lady Warwick the previous week to discuss business affairs. During the course of their discussion she had told him that she had written her memoirs and had been offered a considerable sum of money—"a very considerable sum"—for them. She had told him that a high value had been set upon her proposed book because of certain letters she intended to include.

Du Cros drew a letter out of the envelope and handed it to Lord Albemarle. "This is one of the letters," he said.

Even before he looked at that letter Albemarle must have suspected what was coming. The mention of Lady Warwick and "certain letters" was enough. Those suspicions were dismally confirmed when he saw the Marlborough Club notepaper and the immediately recognizable handwriting. How often, in King Edward's day, had he seen that hasty angular scrawl! The opening words, "My own lovely little Daisy," indicated what kind of letter it must be. He hardly needed to read it, but he did so, and during that reading he was probably already speculating upon what part du Cros was playing in this business and why he had brought the letter to him.

After reading it, he asked if du Cros had seen other letters. Du Cros said he had seen the typed copy of another letter, and from what he had read of it he knew it was of the same nature.

Lord Albemarle said he found it difficult to believe that Lady Warwick, reckless and unconventional though she had been in the past and though now a Socialist, could really face the disgrace of making her love affair public.

Du Cros told him that Frances Warwick knew that publication would "blast" her reputation but claimed she had no alternative because she was so heavily in debt. To convince Albemarle that she really did intend to publish, he then handed to Albemarle the letter she had written to him from Easton Lodge. Du Cros had obviously taken that letter to the interview to make his position in the matter quite clear. He wanted to establish at the very outset that he had had no prior knowledge of Lady Warwick's plan and was not collaborating with her in the project.

However, the point in the letter which must have impressed Albemarle most was the revelation that du Cros was one of Lady Warwick's creditors. This, he may have thought, could mean that du Cros might have some financial interest in the value of the

BEAUTY OF THE MARLBOROUGH HOUSE SET
Frances, Countess of Warwick, called "Daisy."

ARTHUR DU CROS, *Member of Parliament and head of the Dunlop Rubber Corporation, was used as an intermediary between Lady Warwick and Buckingham Palace, and lost £64,000 in the process.*

"DARLING DAISY" *as she was in 1890*
when she begged the Prince of Wales to be her champion
in the Beresford affair.

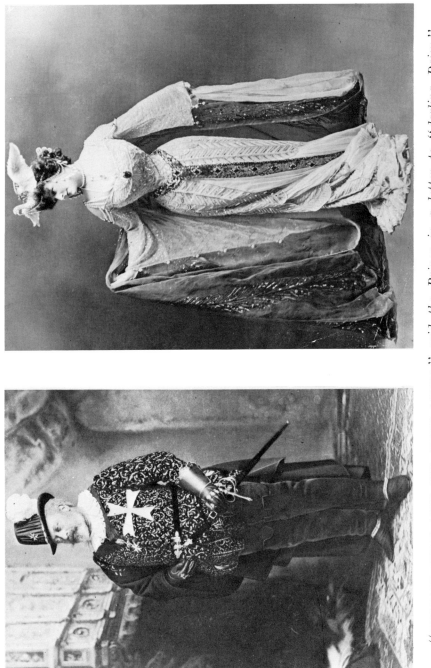

"EVERYONE SEEMS GONE MAD ABOUT ACTING," said the Prince in a letter to "darling Daisy."
Here he is seen costumed for a fancy-dress ball as "Grand Prior of the Order of St. John of Jerusalem,"
and Lady Warwick as "Queen of Assyria."

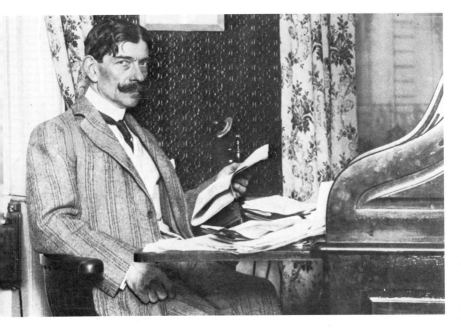

FRANK HARRIS, *the notorious journalist, who told Lady Warwick that her Royal love letters could earn her more than £100,000.*

END OF A ROMANCE
Edward, Prince of Wales, at 57, when "darling Daisy" had become just "a good friend" and he had begun a new liaison with Mrs. Keppel, aged 29.

EDWARDIAN MAMA   *The public, which knew nothing of her private life, saw Lady Warwick (shown here with her second son) as a demure and lovely mother of four handsome children.*

"DYNAMITE IN HIS SAFE"   *Clarence Hatry, the financier who hid the "Darling Daisy" letters, is shown on his yacht with his family before the crash that sent him to jail.*

"MY OWN LOVELY LITTLE DAISY"   *First and last pages of a letter from the Prince of Wales which convinced Arthur du Cros that Lady Warwick's memoirs must not be published.*

SOCIALIST COUNTESS *Turning to politics, Lady Warwick addresses voters at Leamington,*

letters. He also seized upon Lady Warwick's statement that she intended to go to Paris to complete the deal. Why Paris, if she was thinking of selling the book to American publishers? Du Cros explained that a journalist in Paris was helping Frances Warwick to negotiate its sale.

Albemarle agreed with du Cros that there was no other way but to let the King know about the business, despite the fact that His Majesty had so many grave worries on his shoulders at this moment. Unfortunately, King George was again out of London. He had left town for the races at Newmarket and would be staying at the Jockey Club there until Thursday. Yet Albemarle considered the affair of such urgency that immediate action had to be taken; in his private account of this interview du Cros reports Albemarle as saying that it could be necessary to bring the matter to the attention of Lord Stamfordham, King George's secretary, without delay. "I consequently authorised him to make whatever communication he considered necessary."

Albemarle promised to get in touch with du Cros after the King had returned to London and as soon as there was anything further to discuss. He suggested they might meet again on the coming Friday, the day after the King's return and the day when he himself would be again coming up to London from Windsor.

The interview ended on a quietly cordial note. The

manner in which Albemarle expressed his appreciation of the action du Cros had taken apparently made du Cros feel that his moves in the affair were recognized as the public-spirited service of a loyal subject, a service which would not be overlooked or forgotten in the future.

We can take it for granted that Albemarle took the very first opportunity that same day of letting Stamfordham know what was happening. King George's private secretary was fully qualified to assess the situation. He had been Queen Victoria's secretary in the last years of her reign, and would therefore know as much as any man living about Edward's private capers and the extent of his association with Frances Warwick.

So the Beresford letter was copied again—this time by someone on Lord Albemarle's staff, though not photographed—and the copy was placed before Stamfordham along with the news of Lady Warwick's threat. After which Albemarle sent the original of the letter, together with Lady Warwick's letter, back to du Cros.

In my "Darling Daisy" dossier is the covering note he sent with them. It is a model of courtly discretion. Albemarle's main preoccupation was to keep du Cros, and anyone else concerned in the affair, patient and quiet until the Palace had decided what to do. He was also anxious not to excite du Cros into thinking that this Lady Warwick affair could be causing undue alarm at the Palace or was considered as being even particularly urgent. Accordingly, and without, of course, naming the subject to which the letters referred, he wrote:

In the absence from London of one of the most interested "Personages" it was not found possible to make any move in the matter. Even if it was eventually done.

On Thursday the "most interested Personage," King George, returned to London. Du Cros expected that Albemarle would have news for him the following day. But the King went down to Shrewsbury that day to lay the foundation stone of a new library at Shrewsbury School and visit the Royal Agricultural Show. On Saturday the Dowager Queen Alexandra, opening a new park at Wembley, declared herself touched and proud that it should be named after her late husband, King Edward VII.

Du Cros waited through the weekend with mounting impatience, but on Monday when he arrived at his Regent Street office there was a message on his desk. Would he please ring Lord Stamfordham at Victoria 4832? He did so. Could he please come round to St. James's immediately? Stamfordham had at last decided on his course of action.

Lord Stamfordham was a Royal servant in the classic pattern: son of a clergyman, an ex-soldier, icily polite, tall, stern and military-mustached. His years as private secretary to Queen Victoria, followed by his close association with Edward as a King, had been grueling training in the conduct of Royal business. He had learned to be courteous, cautious and suspicious. Above all, suspicious—and suspicious was what he certainly was when on that Monday morning, after his ritual morning ride in Hyde Park, he received du Cros in his office at St. James's Palace.

As it happened, the news of Lady Warwick's activities reached him at a period when, as secretary to the King, Stamfordham was deeply engaged in protecting his Royal master from attacks from all sides. Threat of civil war in Ireland had led the critics of King and Crown to drag those sacred institutions into political argument. So much so that the radical press was now daring to speak with casual contempt of the sovereign and to talk about the advisers around him as aristocratic "hangers-on" at Court. The King was himself so worried about such attacks that he had spoken to the Prime Minister about "the increasing gravity of the situation and the dreadful predicament which would face the Crown if civil war broke out." Added to which, the whole concept of the aristocracy as an elite of high and mighty lords of ancient title or noble service to their King had not yet recovered from the insult it suffered when Mr. Lloyd George had threatened to create a whole army of new peers to vote for his

budget in the House of Lords if the existing heredi-
tary peers attempted to throw it out.

Compared with such immense political dangers,
this sordid little affair of Lady Warwick's might
seem of little account, but Stamfordham well knew
that in the existing circumstances a scandal affecting
the Royal Family and the aristocracy, and one
revealing such corruption and double-dealing
around the Court, would strengthen the enemies of
the Establishment, shock and weaken its supporters,
and could easily be that one "last straw" precipi-
tating a constitutional crisis. Also, Stamfordham
would be acutely conscious that any attack on King
Edward's memory would desperately hurt King
George, who had adored his father unquestioningly
and "next idolatry."

Being so fully aware of the ins and outs of the
situation, Stamfordham quite possibly suspected
that Lady Warwick had deliberately timed her attack to come just at the time when the Palace was
least able to make a strong retort. He might also
have wondered just how disinterested du Cros really
was.

Dispensing with preliminaries, he boldly went
straight to the heart of the matter and asked what du
Cros' interest was in the affair.

Justifiably, du Cros was aggrieved by the question. He explained that he had approached Lord
Albemarle and the Palace because he felt someone

ought to know what Lady Warwick was planning to do, and because he felt that in the interests of the nation and Royal Family she ought to be prevented from doing it.

Well and good. But why was it that Lady Warwick had revealed this "secret work" to Mr. Arthur du Cros? The hint was obvious. Lord Stamfordham now knew that du Cros was one of Lady Warwick's creditors and he was really asking du Cros if he had been pressing her for money.

Du Cros explained that she did owe him a lot of money but he had not been demanding repayment of the debt. His private record of the conversation records that Stamfordham's questioning on this point stung him to declare: "Furthermore, I should find it objectionable to be repaid with any money raised in the manner Lady Warwick proposes to raise it."

From that moment the interview seems to have gone more smoothly. Lord Stamfordham had apparently got the measure of Mr. du Cros and believed what he said. The M.P. was patently not a party to the plot, not an ally of Lady Warwick. At this point Stamfordham must have realized how useful du Cros could be to the Palace. Like a kind of "neutral power," he could be employed to keep contact between the warring parties and thus save the Royal Household from having with Lady Warwick that close contact which might be dangerous and would certainly be distasteful.

Yet this first interview with Stamfordham came to what du Cros must have felt was a rather inconclusive end. Stamfordham gave him no indication whether the news of what was happening had been told to King George, who had now left London again, this time for a week's state visit to Scotland. Lord Stamfordham promised, however, to contact du Cros if and when necessary.

Despite Stamfordham's quite genial leavetaking, du Cros must have left St. James's very disquieted. The interview had brought home to him forcefully a realization of the situation Lady Warwick had steered him into. Indeed, it could look as though he, Arthur du Cros, M.P., was actually acting as an agent for a wicked woman trying to extort silence money from the Royal Family. Probably he also had in his mind something he had not as yet disclosed to Albemarle or Stamfordham, something that could arouse the gravest suspicions against him. He had so far avoided telling them the name of that "journalist in Paris" who was collaborating with Lady Warwick. What might they think if and when they discovered that man was Frank Harris, the very man Arthur du Cros had himself employed? Then indeed it would look as though he were up to his neck in the plot.

It was almost certainly because of such worries

that he now decided he must take some positive action on his own account and, in so doing, establish his innocence.

Lady Warwick, he remembered, had told him that up to the moment when she revealed to him the project of publishing her memoirs only two other people in the world knew of her intentions. One, obviously, was Frank Harris. Who could be the other? Almost inevitably her solicitor.

He went to see that gentleman, Sir Henry Paget-Cooke, in the solicitor's office at Old Square, Lincoln's Inn, the following day. This interview turned out to be a crucial and somewhat surprising one in these early negotiations, and du Cros kept a full record of it.

Yes, Sir Henry did know of Lady Warwick's plan to publish her memoirs. In fact, he confided to du Cros, it had been a matter of some argument between them. He had advised her not to do it. She had insisted. Consequently, he had refused to act for her in the matter. He told du Cros, in strictest confidence, that he had in fact been very much exercised in his mind over the affair. He had felt increasingly that it was his duty to inform the Crown of Lady Warwick's intentions. But Lady Warwick was his client, to whom he had the legal obligations of a solicitor. Consequently, he had been thinking of putting the facts before the Lord Chancellor and asking his advice on the question of privilege and on whether, in the circumstances, he would be within his legal rights in communicating with Lord Stamford-ham himself. Du Cros' timely action had, however, saved him from the necessity of doing that, and now he need no longer consider the rather distasteful prospect of, as it were, breaking faith with a client.

One wonders how long Frances Warwick had been waiting for her solicitor to do the very thing he had been so chary of doing. Perhaps she had been waiting impatiently for Sir Henry to let the Palace know, and when at last she lost patience she had turned to du Cros as second-best intermediary.

Let us, however, see what Lady Warwick has to say about this interview at Lincoln's Inn. In the statement he later prepared for the King's solicitors, Arthur du Cros says quite definitely that Sir Henry knew about Lady Warwick's plan to write her memoirs and had refused to act for her in the matter. In a note she scribbled and underlined on the margin of the du Cros statement, she denies that Sir Henry or any other lawyer knew of her plan.

This makes it out that Sir Henry was a liar. Unfortunately for Frances Warwick, she had a shaky memory, and only a couple of minutes after scribbling that marginal note she proved that it was not Sir Henry but she who was the liar. For on the very next page of the du Cros statement, where he describes receiving from her eventually *three* copies of Edward's letters, she says that one of the letters was in possession of Sir Henry.

While du Cros was engaging in his own inquiries, things were taking place of which he could not be aware. Behind the apparent calm of the Palace there was feverish legal activity. Stamfordham, after discussing the matter with the King, had already set in motion an operation planned to silence Lady Warwick—or at least keep her quiet long enough for some final settlement to be made.

Three days after his interview with Stamfordham, du Cros found another message on his desk.

Mr Charles Russell, solicitor, 37 Norfolk Street, Strand, is very anxious to get into communication with you immediately *re Lord Stamfordham and Lady Warwick. He has called, and telephoned twice since.*

Du Cros called at once on the Hon. Charles Russell, solicitor to King George, and was asked, once again, to tell his side of the story.

He did so, repeating to the King's solicitor all that he had told Albemarle and Stamfordham. Then Mr. Russell took up the conversation. What he said at that interview reveals that at last the Palace, now legally advised, had begun the process of making use of du Cros as a "neutral" intermediary—or rather as a scout, pushing him forward into enemy territory to estimate the real strength and dangers. From du Cros' record it is obvious that he had managed to convince the solicitor, as he had tried to convince Stamfordham, that he was not acting in concert with Lady Warwick in the hope of her raising money and paying her debt to him.

Yet it must have been clear to a legal mind, if not yet to du Cros', that Frances Warwick had called du Cros in not because she wanted advice about publishing the letters but because she had other plans in mind for turning those letters into money. And it is completely certain that Russell had asked du Cros to call at his office that day for a very particular purpose. By some means the Palace had to "talk" with the enemy. A very delicate and somewhat dangerous question had to be got through to Lady Warwick. Put more bluntly and brutally than the King's solicitor would ever dare to put it, the question was: How much did Lady Warwick want for her silence? Du Cros, the "neutral," was the ideal instrument for conveying that question discreetly to Lady Warwick. Though, in priming du Cros for this task, the King's solicitor had to avoid using words which could be construed as meaning that the Palace was prepared to be a party to blackmail.

Mr. Russell found this easy. He recognized that du Cros was eager, and perhaps proud, to be employed by the Palace as an intermediary. Du Cros readily agreed with Mr. Russell's suggestion that he should see Lady Warwick again, that he should again try to persuade her to drop the idea of publishing the letters.

Du Cros said he had not much hope that he could persuade her to do that. If he failed, what then?

This was the crucial moment of the interview, and the solicitor must have felt the need of framing his words carefully. Du Cros records that Russell then suggested that if Lady Warwick still insisted on publishing the letters, du Cros should try *"to ascertain the monetary value she attached to them with a view to their purchase."*

Those quoted words are the exact words du Cros later used to describe Mr. Russell's request when he prepared his statement of events for the King's solicitors. When Mr. Russell vetted that statement he deleted the final words: *"with a view to their purchase."* At first glance the deletion seems mere legal quibbling, but actually those six words were nastily significant.

Later, when he was reviewing the part he had played in the Lady Warwick affair and sorting through some of the documents, Arthur du Cros came across the deletion the solicitor had made on his statement and he scribbled in the margin: "This deletion made by Mr C Russell, but it is not justified." So it appears that du Cros was utterly convinced Mr. Russell had suggested that the Palace might purchase the letters. But the King's solicitor would naturally not want such a suggestion in any document. The remotest hint that the Palace could contemplate *buying* the letters could not be allowed in print anywhere. No, that was too close to the bone —too close to the idea that the Palace was considering paying "hush money."

However, Mr. Russell did go as near as any solicitor, let alone a solicitor to the King, could go in asking Arthur du Cros to find out how much Lady Warwick wanted for her silence. Du Cros took the hint. The interview had made him see suddenly and clearly that he had been dragged inch by inch into the role of negotiator in a transaction only the merest shade away from outright blackmail. He must have resented it, but must also have realized that, having gone so far, he could not now draw back.

Consequently, he went immediately to 37 Eaton Square. Lady Warwick, who had waited for so long for news of what he might have succeeded in doing with her letter, must have been glad to see him. She had already postponed her July 7 appointment in Paris with Harris in the hope that du Cros would be able to tell her how the Palace was reacting, and when he told her that he had discussed the matter with Albemarle and Stamfordham and the King's solicitor she was anxious to hear what they had said.

Mr. Russell, said du Cros, had asked him to strongly advise Lady Warwick against publishing the letters or writing anything at all about her association with King Edward.

Frances Warwick was not, of course, surprised to hear that, and when du Cros continued, telling her that the two courtiers had agreed with him that such an action would disgrace her utterly, she pointed out that it would not be a greater disgrace than bankruptcy.

This gave du Cros the cue to lead up to the inquiry the Palace had asked him to make. After hinting that it might be possible for Lady Warwick to avoid both disgraces, he said that it might be possible to raise money without publishing the letters.

When he said that, she must have realized that at last things were going the way she had planned.

What, he asked her, did she think the letters were worth? In sheer hard cash? He pointed out that he was not now discussing how much their value might be if published, but how much she would think they were worth if some interested party suggested that she sell them privately instead of publishing them.

Yes, this was undoubtedly what she had waited for. The reply she made came so readily as to indicate that she had waited for the question for quite a while.

Was Mr. du Cros making a business proposal? she asked.

"She was ready to consider a business proposal from me," reported du Cros in his description of the interview, "which however she would not be able to conclude without the concurrence of Mr Frank Harris."

Refusing, however, to be sidetracked into any discussion of Frank Harris' interest in the letters, du Cros persisted in his attempt to get a figure from her. At last she gave him one.

"I gathered that the lowest sum she would entertain would be one which would free her from her liabilities, which she estimated at £85,000."

Lady Warwick was obviously now confident that things were going her way. For she followed up this bold demand for £85,000 with a warning that "the matter could not be stayed."

. . There was little time left for any discussion, she told du Cros. Less than four days, in fact. She was due to meet Mr. Harris in Paris on Tuesday to finalize the agreement. She could not wait any longer than that.

Du Cros told her that he would be seeing Mr. Russell again and asked her to lend him copies of some of the letters that he could show to the King's solicitor. She gave him two.

It was by now too late in the day for du Cros to catch Russell at his office, but early the following morning he went round to Norfolk Street. He had already decided on a plan of his own.

First he reported that Lady Warwick had set the value of the letters at the high figure of £85,000. Then he told Russell what he proposed to do. As

Lady Warwick had said that she could not conclude any business negotiation without the concurrence of her journalist collaborator, he had decided to go to Paris himself and meet them both there.

There were two reasons why du Cros would feel that it was necessary for him to be present in Paris when Frances Warwick met Frank Harris. The first was that he was frightened, knowing the way Harris worked and his notorious power to charm women, that the journalist would bully her into signing on the spot an agreement binding her to the publication of her memoirs. The second reason was that only by meeting Harris face to face could he hope to find out the monetary value Harris really put on the letters. In du Cros' opinion, that value could be arrived at by simple subtraction of one figure from another. One figure was the amount which Lady Warwick's memoirs could be expected to earn if the letters *were* included. The other figure was the amount expected if the letters were *not* included. Surely, argued du Cros, the difference between those figures was the logical monetary value of the letters to Lady Warwick.

In his report of the interview du Cros wrote: "I informed Mr Russell of my intention, in which he concurred."

Of course Russell concurred. The King's solicitor could not be other than delighted at du Cros' offer to go to Paris. It saved the Palace, once again, from getting too close to an unpleasant matter. The journalist in Paris who was collaborating with Lady Warwick in writing her memoirs would accept du Cros' presence at the discussion as quite logical, in view of the fact that du Cros was a creditor of hers and thus had a legitimate interest in her finances.

Perhaps du Cros realized why Russell so readily accepted his offer. By acting as a go-between, du Cros gave the Palace a chance to remain in the background, discreetly removed from what was rapidly developing into a sordid blackmail transaction.

That morning he sent a message to Lady Warwick telling her that he intended to go to Paris to discuss the matter with Frank Harris in her presence. He asked that they call on him at the Ritz Hotel and baited his invitation with the hint that he now felt sure some financial arrangement agreeable to Lady Warwick could be arrived at.

The reply came back that Lady Warwick and "her agent" would call on Mr. du Cros at the Ritz on the evening of Monday, July 13.

That Monday-evening appointment was not kept. The meeting was postponed until the following day. The reason is not explained in any of the notes, letters or documents in my possession, but from what did happen at the postponed conference a likely reason for the postponement would seem to be that Lady Warwick and Frank Harris wanted that evening free to discuss in detail the plan of campaign they would adopt when they confronted du Cros. So it was that on the morning of Tuesday, July 14, 1914, Frances, Countess of Warwick, Mr. Arthur du Cros, M.P., and Mr. Frank Harris met to do battle at the Ritz Hotel in Paris.

Up to this point in the story I have been able, by use of Arthur du Cros' notes, the documents unearthed in Switzerland and information collected from other sources and from people concerned in the negotiations, to give a full account of the interviews between Lady Warwick, du Cros, Albemarle, Stamfordham and Russell. But the documentation on the Harris interview is even richer, providing a blow-by-blow account of a conference which was not only a vital one in the Warwick affair but also surely the most outrageous one ever conducted under the luxurious roof of the Ritz.

5

A ROW AT THE RITZ

It was a few minutes after eleven o'clock on the morning of Tuesday, July 14, 1914, when Arthur du Cros, waiting impatiently in his suite at the Ritz in Paris, was told that a Mr. Frank Harris had arrived and was waiting downstairs. Du Cros invited his visitor upstairs. Harris refused to come up. "I'll wait downstairs," he said. Harris, an old hand in the business of shady and near-criminal intrigue, and far less ingenuous than du Cros, obviously had suspicions which du Cros would have considered outrageous. Harris did not relish the prospect of conducting the kind of interview he had in mind in a private room where a witness might be hidden in a cupboard or in an adjoining room. At that time the strictly

(*165*)

honorable du Cros would never have believed it possible for such men as Stamfordham and Russell to resort to such methods. But Harris, as du Cros was to discover later, was wiser than he: the Palace had already put private detectives on the job.

By the time du Cros came down Harris had swaggered into one of the public rooms and was standing at a window, his back to the room, staring out into the Place Vendôme, his body braced into the forceful leg-straddling Napoleonic stance he customarily adopted to compensate for his lack of height.

He turned slowly when du Cros came in, greeted him by his first name, apologized for being late and made some jocular remark about their being at last "in business again." The words set the tone of what Arthur du Cros always recalled as an unpleasant and at times near to humiliating interview. It was some years since the two men had last met. There had been, one of du Cros' sons tells me, "a mighty row" between them concerning some writing or editing Harris was doing for the M.P. in his constituency and they had broken off relations violently. Harris was now fifty-eight, but he had not changed a great deal since du Cros last saw him. Except that perhaps there was now about him a hint of seediness, some faint odor of shabbiness seeping through the flamboyant façade despite the undoubtedly expensive suit, the pearl-studded cravat and the dandified yellow spats. Du Cros noticed with distaste that although the heavy watch chain draped across the bow of the embroidered waistcoat was of gold, the knob of the malacca cane was of silver, and slightly tarnished at that. Harris was a little man, but did not give the impression of being so. The bulk of his body, the enormous chest and arms short but stalwart as a prizefighter's gave him an aspect of brutal physical power; the high Cuban heels he habitually wore gave him extra inches.

Harris cheated not only about his height, but about all manner of things. His birth, for instance. He claimed to have been born in Galway, also in Tenby, also in Brighton. His parents had given him the names "James Thomas," but he had adopted the name "Frank."

His face was swarthy and heavy, notable for big ugly ears and a cap of thick hair growing low enough over his brow to give him what was described as an "almost Neanderthal" appearance. Yet his fierce energy and tireless employment of varied talents had overcome any social disability his appearance might have caused, and he had clambered to the front ranks of literary London, numbering among his friends such men as Oscar Wilde, Aubrey Beardsley and Max Beerbohm, and among his close acquaintances even such eminences as H. G. Wells and Bernard Shaw, though the latter described him as "a ruffian and a monster" who had "quarrelled with everyone except Shakespeare," whom Harris vener-

ated. He was also credited with the power of evoking
the passionate desire of women, although as he
boasted so much about his sexual conquests in *My
Life and Loves* one begins to suspect that he probably created that reputation himself. However, such
a reputation can sometimes run like a virus among
womenfolk, and some who were infected by the Harris legend claimed that his booming voice "like the
rustling of iron leaves" seemed "to hypnotise you
. . . to grip you."

At one time he had been a brilliantly successful
London editor, had lived luxuriously in a Park Lane
house and had even entertained hopes of becoming
Prime Minister! But at the time of the meeting in the
Ritz his star, both literary and sexual, was setting.
Not so much the saucy scandals he propagated but
rather his shady financial deals had moved society to
cross him off the invitation lists, and he had found it
necessary to sneak out of London to Paris, in which
city he could still for a while strut around with the
manner of a powerful literary tycoon.

This, then, was the man, desperately desirous of
fame and even more in need of cash, who had
suddenly got his hands latched around what he would
describe as "a valuable literary property." How
binding was his agreement with Lady Warwick,
whether any actual contract had been signed, neither
he nor she ever revealed. It is almost certain that
there was no contract at all. In fact, everything

seems to indicate that the haughty and aristocratic
Countess of Warwick, outwardly so gracious and
ingenuous, was two tricks ahead of Harris all the
time, using him merely as the ogre she could drag out
to reinforce her threat of publication. If, then, there
was no contract, we can imagine that Harris would
fight all the harder to maintain his grip on the
publishing project. This explains the bitterness of
the battle waged at the Ritz that July morning.

Somewhat taken aback when he saw that Harris
was alone, du Cros asked why Lady Warwick was
not here. Harris shrugged this off, telling him that
she was on her way. Probably she had overslept a
little after a late night, and the laugh with which he
accompanied this opinion was nicely calculated to
suggest that the two of them had been making a
night of it in Paris, though du Cros knew Harris too
well to pay much attention to such innuendoes.

Du Cros thought it would be best to wait for her
before any discussion began, but Harris, assuring
him that she would be along soon enough, suggested
that, as he was in any case acting as her "agent" in
the matter, they might as well proceed. After all, he
had the power to discuss any terms on her behalf. He
asked du Cros what was his interest in the business.

Harris always took it for granted that no one did
anything without self-interest, and he was sure his
former employer had a personal axe to grind. After
all, he was a financier, a politician and one of Lady

Warwick's creditors.

Du Cros replied that his only personal interest was to advise Lady Warwick on a proper course of action.

Harris expressed himself pleased. That was his interest, too. They both had a stake in the dear woman: he as a writer, du Cros as someone she owed money to.

Du Cros said he did not see it that way at all. His intention was to prevent her doing something foolish. He was advising her, in her own interest and in the interest of her family, not to include certain letters in her memoirs.

Harris could hardly let that euphemism "certain letters" pass. Bluntly he described them as "dear old Edward's letters" and then declared that those letters *were* the memoirs. They were the one priceless feature amid what would otherwise be a lot of high-society chitchat. Edward's letters would "make" the book, and make Frances a fortune.

Money, retorted du Cros, could hardly compensate for the damage she would do to herself and to others by publishing such a scandal.

Money, argued Harris, compensated for most things. Du Cros, he said, well knew what a fix Frances was in. What alternative did du Cros propose? Frances had told him that du Cros had an idea she might make a deal and sell the letters instead of publishing them. Was du Cros the "interested party" who wanted to buy them?

According to du Cros' account of the interview, this was the moment he chose to tell Harris, "I have consulted a very old friend of the late King Edward and I am not, therefore, acting alone in this matter."

Harris assumed a scornful attitude, asking du Cros if it were not true that this "very old friend of King Edward's" had now had a word with King George, and that the Royal Family were rallying round to keep the story of Edward's "darling Daisy" out of print. How much, he asked, were they prepared to put up?

It must have been a relief to du Cros that Lady Warwick appeared at this moment. Harris welcomed her with a great display of gallantry, addressing her as "Frances, darling!" and praising her for making, as always, a perfectly timed entrance. Trying generally to take social command of the scene, he dragged a chair forward for her and summoned a waiter to take an order for drinks from Mr. du Cros. He then laid his curly-brimmed bowler and malacca cane on a side table and sank back in a chair, stretching his short thick legs to the footstool, upon which he crossed his high-heeled shoes.

Entrenched in this insolent position, he returned to his attack on du Cros. Frances, he said, had already told du Cros how much he, Harris, believed her book could earn. At least £125,000. That was a conservative estimate. Mr. du Cros must realize that it was not merely a matter of royalties on the book. There would be serial rights from newspapers and magazines. Foreign rights. All kinds of possibilities.

Du Cros agreed that there were indeed "other possibilities." There were the possibilities of the harm the book could do and the disgrace Lady Warwick would call down on herself by putting her name to it. At this Harris taxed du Cros with first threatening Lady Warwick with bankruptcy and then warning her of what she would suffer in her attempts to avoid it.

Du Cros heatedly refuted the allegation that he was threatening her with bankruptcy. Nor, he said, did she stand in any fear of it if she took advantage of a likely opportunity of disposing of the letters in some other way.

Did du Cros mean by selling them to an "interested party"? Harris asked. How much would such people be prepared to pay?

Du Cros did not reply directly to these questions. He pointed out that Lady Warwick had named the figure she had in mind: £85,000. That was far too high, but it could at least serve as a starting-off point for any eventual discussion with people considering the purchase of the letters.

Harris dismissed this figure contemptuously. Frances, he said, had been foolish to talk in such terms without asking his advice. The only compensation she and he could accept for *not* publishing the letters was the amount they could earn by publishing them—namely, £125,000.

There was not the slightest hope of anyone paying as much as that, said du Cros.

In any case, said Harris, he had now advised Frances to stick out for £125,000 and not to accept a penny less.

Lady Warwick, argued du Cros, had said that her only desire was to raise enough to clear her debts. He turned to her, obviously hoping, by bringing her into the discussion, to prevent Harris from assuming complete command. That, he reminded her, was what she had told him the previous Thursday.

Harris interrupted. Frances had told him the same. He understood that she was now prepared to sell rather than to publish. He could not prevent her from doing that, and he would not stand in her way, providing she was sufficiently compensated and, of course, kept to her agreement with him.

When du Cros asked him what that agreement was, Harris replied that she had agreed to pay him a fee for his work on the book.

"That fee, I understand, is £5,000?" asked du Cros.

Yes, it was, said Harris. Plus, of course, a ten-percent royalty on the sales of the book. That applied, however, only *if* the letters were included in the book.

And if the letters were *not* included?

Ten thousand, plus royalties.

Ten thousand pounds. Shocked, du Cros pointed out that this was twice as much.

Of course it was, said Harris. That was only fair. He had to protect his interests. He must be adequately paid for his work, and he had to take into account that without those "lovely little Daisy" letters the book could not sell half as well.

In that case, said du Cros, he must advise Lady Warwick not to publish any book at all.

In that case, said Harris, Frances would have to pay him £15,000.

Du Cros turned a questioning gaze on Lady Warwick. She nodded to confirm that Harris had correctly stated the terms of her bargain with him.

Harris was still arguing that he had done a lot of work on the book and could not afford to work for nothing, but du Cros ignored him. Addressing Lady Warwick directly, he told her that in the circumstances he could only advise that she agree to a reasonable settlement. He suggested that as she was so committed to Mr. Harris she should go ahead and publish her memoirs, but not destroy her reputation and dishonor her name by including King Edward's letters.

Harris interrupted with a remark that she would thus lose a lot of money, but du Cros argued this was not so. It might be that her memoirs might earn less without the sensation of the letters, but she would be more than compensated for that loss by the considerable sum she would get by selling the letters.

Harris again turned to the question of the amount the "interested parties" might pay for the letters. What would du Cros say was a "considerable sum"?

"At a guess, I should say around half the £125,-000 you talk about," said du Cros bluntly.

Harris treated this reply with a display of anger and described the offer as "pitiable."

Du Cros again addressed himself directly to Lady Warwick. Such a sum, he told her, plus the amount she would earn with her memoirs would meet all her obligations.

But she shook her head and said she had to agree with Mr. Harris that the figure was far too low.

"How much too low?" asked du Cros. "I am not, of course, in a position to make a firm offer here and now, but I should like to establish some basis for negotiation. If I were able to suggest £75,000 . . ."

"No, Mr. du Cros. That is less than I can accept . . . far less.

It could not be "far less," du Cros insisted. It was only £10,000 less than the £85,000 she had suggested herself the previous Thursday.

But that £85,000, she now said, had not included what she must pay Mr. Harris for his work and assistance.

This seems to be the moment Harris had been awaiting. It was the moment he chose to make the decisive offer he had been keeping up his sleeve.

"Frances," he exclaimed, "we're wasting our time." He faced du Cros. "You're only beating the air, du Cros," he said brutally. "Let's cut out all this cant about names and honor and 'interested parties.' Let's face up to the fact that this is a business proposition. What Frances has to sell is something of market value. What you and your people fail to realize is that the deal's as good as fixed in America."

He turned to Lady Warwick.

"Listen, Frances," he said, "I'll show you how confident I am of the success of your book. If you will agree here and now to include the letters in it, then I will agree to cut my fee by half. So you will pay me only £2,500 instead of £5,000. I am sure the royalties will soon repay me for that. That shows you how sure I am of the book being a success."

It also showed just how desperately Harris was depending on getting any cash at all.

Harris must have thought that his offer, coming at the moment when du Cros was haggling about the price of the letters, was perfectly timed to make Lady Warwick clinch the deal. Actually, it came at the right moment for her to do the opposite. Encouraged by Harris' openly declared confidence in the book's possibilities, she now could make her final demand.

Turning to du Cros, she asked him to believe her when she said that she really would rather sell the letters than publish them. But she could not sell them for less than she had asked: £85,000, plus, of course, the £15,000 she would have to pay Mr. Harris as she had agreed.

Harris protested. She was, he said, "throwing money away" . . . throwing thousands away!

She ignored those arguments. "That is my final offer, Mr. du Cros."

Du Cros refused to commit himself. For his part, he still thought the sum was excessive, he said, but in any case he could certainly not say anything more until he had had further consultation in London.

"We can't wait forever, du Cros," said Harris as, deflated and sulky, he picked up his hat and gloves.

Du Cros promised to get in touch with Lady Warwick as soon as he had discussed the matter further in London. Would she be at Easton?

Yes, she would, but she warned him that there was now very little time. The matter must be concluded, either in London or in America, and quickly.

On this note the interview ended and Harris marched out of the room. But he waited for Lady Warwick in the entrance of the Ritz, ostensibly to accompany her back to her hotel off the Champs-Elysées, but obviously determined to continue his arguments when they were out of earshot of du Cros.

Du Cros went back to his suite to relax and study the situation. A tetchy man at the best of times and accustomed to getting his own way, du Cros must have found it a strenuous exercise to restrain his anger under the galling irritation of Harris' bluster and vulgarity, yet by and large he was not depressed by the way things had gone.

In his view, the most promising and significant feature of the conference had been Lady Warwick's refusal of Harris' offer to forgo £2,500 of his fee. This refusal had convinced du Cros that she really would prefer to sell the letters, and he felt that this preference was something he must seize upon and exploit. Accordingly, he drafted a cable to the King's solicitor, telling him that although Lady Warwick was still refusing to lower her demands, he believed the position could be dealt with. By this he meant, he says in his notes, the purchase of the letters. He therefore asked Russell to arrange an immediate meeting with Lord Stamfordham.

Having sent the cable, he packed his bag and left Paris, hoping that when he reached London he would soon have an interview at St. James's and then go to Easton to see Lady Warwick. But, most unexpectedly, he came face to face with her again that same day.

He was promenading the deck of the Folkestone boat, taking the air of the bright July day, when he saw her sitting on a deck chair in a quiet corner, a small and rakish-looking black velvet toque pulled down to protect her hair from the strong Channel breeze and a costly traveling cape heavily trimmed with fur slung, carelessly as a rug, across her knees.

Open on her lap was a French novel, *Nouvelles Féminités*, a paper-backed volume from the collected works of Marcel Prévost. But she was not reading. She was staring moodily out to sea.

Du Cros must have welcomed this unplanned encounter. To him it would seem an excellent opportunity to tackle Lady Warwick again and, without Frank Harris' presence and interference, cement her resolve to sell the letters.

She looked up, expressed her surprise at the coincidence of their meeting and told him he was just the person she was thinking about.

He was pleased to hear that, and said he hoped she had been thinking over his advice.

She had indeed, she said, but if du Cros did not think the King would pay £100,000 . . .

He interrupted her, pointing out that no one had said anything about "the King" paying. Impatiently she said that was, in any case, what it amounted to, but du Cros insisted that the King's name should not be dragged into the discussion.

But who else, she asked, would want to buy the letters? He expressed the opinion that in the circumstances it was quite likely some public-spirited person might be prepared to buy them to prevent the dangerous scandal of publication.

Perhaps this was the moment when there was born in Frances Warwick's mind a belief that she was in an even more powerful position than she had first imagined. Perhaps it was at this moment that she realized that even if the Royal Family could not be frightened into paying "hush money" there were always others who would—out of patriotism or loyalty, or for no other reason than to render the present King meritorious service. One can imagine her resting the gaze of those dark-blue eyes reflectively on du Cros as this idea took shape in her mind.

Du Cros' account of the conversation on the Folkestone boat indicates that this was the occasion when she first put into words the defense for her actions which she later repeated in a letter to du Cros. Her defense was that the £100,000 she was demanding was far less than what her association with "dear Edward" had actually cost her. When du Cros expressed the opinion that it seemed sordid to count the cost of a "friendship" in terms of thousands of pounds, she replied that, unfortunately, one did get sordid when up to one's ears in debt. "Dear Edward" had been ruinous in money matters: not wickedly so, but just incapable of appreciating what a financial strain he imposed upon the friends who entertained him and provided him with sumptuous hospitality.

Certainly it was on the Folkestone boat that du Cros suggested that she was possibly exaggerating her financial worries. Did she really owe as much as £85,000? When she said she did, he asked her to do something. Would she, when she got back to London, make out a list of her liabilities and let him have a copy?

She asked him what purpose there would be in doing that. He replied that it would give him a clear picture of the situation and would help him in any later discussions he might have.

When she promised to do this, he then asked her to do something far more pointed. Would she also put into writing that she was prepared to sell the letters for such a sum as would meet her present liabilities?

We can see what du Cros was after. He was trying to stabilize the "monetary value" of the letters as much as possible, and was probably even then thinking that if some of those liabilities might be reduced in some way, then the sum demanded from the Palace or from any other "interested party" might be less excessive.

As it turned out, she prepared the list of her liabilities before they reached London. She joined du Cros in his compartment on the train to London and told him she had written it.

From between the pages of the Marcel Prévost novel she drew out a folded piece of paper. It was her receipted bill from the Hotel Avenida, off the Champs-Elysées. The total—including her room at 18 francs, lunch, citronnades, etc.—was a mere 56 francs 85 centimes, but the figures she had penciled on the other side were vastly bigger. She tore the bill down the fold and handed one half to du Cros.

This piece of paper survives as a most revealing scrap of evidence in the Lady Warwick affair. Nothing could better illustrate the woman's disastrous incapacity to deal with anything even remotely approaching financial calculation, and that meticulous man-of-affairs Arthur du Cros often described later his feeling of shocked helplessness when Frances presented him with this attempt at a debtor's balance sheet. Nevertheless, he preserved the amateur effort—surely one of the oddest documents ever to find its way into a financier's file—and eventually it took its place in the cache of "Darling Daisy" documents.

He had to agree that she had done as he had asked her. To the limit of her capabilities, she had jotted down her debts in what one customarily describes as "round figures." Round they undoubtedly were. And big. As a man of business, he was exasperated that she seemed uncertain even about some debts amounting to teens of thousands, and he was quite taken aback by her hint that the debt to him, the one which according to her had actually precipitated her financial crisis and about which they had talked so much, might perhaps be more that £16,000. Knowing what we do now, it is easy to see what she was getting at. Taking clearer shape in her mind at that moment was the hope that if du Cros really was a loyal subject of his King, he might be prepared to shoulder a larger proportion of her debts than a mere £16,000.

But the thing that most irked du Cros was her insistence that the "poisonous" Harris should be included among her creditors and must be paid his fee according to the terms he had laid down at the conference at the Ritz: £10,000 for writing her memoirs *without* Edward's letters. Indeed, when du Cros studied this "balance sheet" later that evening in his Regent Street office and formulated his own plan to silence Lady Warwick and appease her creditors, he realized that Lady Warwick's literary enterprise had by now grown into one of her bigger liabilities and the expenses she had incurred in its pursuit already accounted for a considerable proportion of her total debts. For, in addition to the £10,000 she owed Harris, she owed other thousands of pounds to people who had helped or advised her in the negotiations. There were, for instance, the fees due to her solicitor, Sir Henry Paget-Cooke, for his services. One can understand how angry du Cros was months later when, despite this written evidence filed in his office, she blandly denied that she had ever consulted Sir Henry on the matter of dear Edward's letters.

She also told du Cros during that conversation on the boat train that she must pay the traveling expenses of the friend who had taken the letters across the Channel to show to Harris. But, despite his questions, she refused to tell him, then or later, who this friend was.

"That's the lot, Mr. du Cros," she murmured.

"Calculated to a penny."

To a penny! Even Arthur du Cros had to smile, though wryly, at that. Whenever he told the story of that financial conference on the boat train, he recalled, with that same wry smile, this phrase of hers.

That reluctant smile, that slight softening of the long-nosed financial face, is probably what emboldened Frances Warwick there and then to put into words the nice little hope that had dawned in her calculating head during their earlier talk on the deck of the Folkestone boat. So while du Cros pondered those "round figures" written on the back of the hotel bill, she again flipped open the Marcel Prévost novel, searched for a page with blank space enough for writing on, chose the title page and began scribbling.

"I have an idea," she said, "that might help the situation."

He watched and waited while, with her swift pencil, she covered all the blank space around the title, then turned the page and wrote on the other side. She tore out the page and handed it across to him.

Here it was at last. Now she had put into black and white her hope that Arthur du Cros might act as her knight errant. At first glance the scribbled note seemed no more than a sketchily outlined suggestion of how he could rescue her from her financial plight. But actually it was a blatant invitation for him to plunge in, patriotic and loyal and public-spirited;

an invitation to him to assume the major role in preserving the good name of the Royal Family and, incidentally, take upon his own shoulders the major burden of Frances Warwick's debts. This, he realized, was the real core of the proposals she now put before him. He was being asked not only to let her debt to him rest in abeyance but also to treat with other creditors on her behalf. He, she argued as he read the note, could deal with those people better than she could. He might be able to settle those debts at a lower figure.

It was, he had to agree, feasible that a resolute financier could get a reduction on the bills. But he knew well enough that Frances Warwick did not really care a jot how Arthur du Cros came out of that bargaining. All she wanted to do was to toss the bulk of those vexatious debts into his lap, and if he was a sufficiently patriotic Tory to consider an opportunity of serving his King a satisfactory bonus for such a financial sacrifice, well, she was generously prepared to afford him that opportunity.

That, in any case, was how du Cros saw it as, in the lonely silence of his Regent Street office late that night, he wrote his own summary of her suggestions and prepared the financial plan which he intended to put before the King's advisers. But even on the boat train, even when he was rather dejectedly promising Frances Warwick that he would do what he could, already the realization must have been dawning upon him that somehow, somewhere, the negotiations had taken a turn in which it seemed that his loyal service to his King and Country might prove not only an exhausting enterprise but an expensive one as well.

By now the train was steaming into Charing Cross. He reminded her that he had asked her also to give him a note declaring her willingness to sell the letters for such a sum as would dispose of these debts.

She had not written it. She considered that the list of debts she had jotted down was in itself sufficient to imply that she would sell at such a figure. But she had written something else that she felt might help Mr. du Cros in his negotiations with the interested parties. She handed to him a handwritten sheet. It was nothing more nor less than an ultimatum.

This document was later given by du Cros to the King's solicitors, and eventually it became "Exhibit C.R.1" in the King's Bench Division of the High Court of Justice when the Palace resorted to law to stop Lady Warwick from publishing Edward's letters. Consequently, it is a document missing from my dossier of the Lady Warwick affair. Fortunately, however, it is quoted in another document—the affidavit sworn on July 29, 1914, by the King's solicitor himself, the Hon. Charles Russell. From it we learn that Frances Warwick informed du Cros of her final plans for Frank Harris: namely, that he should leave shortly for New York with her autobiography, including the letters, and after publication should sell the letters separately. Lady Warwick reckoned on making some £200,000 from this transaction.

The train had come to a halt and Lady Warwick had already beckoned a porter by the time du Cros had read this document and folded it together with the half-sheet of hotel bill and the flyleaf of the novel.

She took her leave of him, telling him that she was going down to Easton the following day and expressing the hope that she would have news from him very soon. Then, her elegant traveling cape slung loosely over her shoulders, Frances, Countess of Warwick, walked graciously down the platform behind the porter who was trundling her baggage and clearing a path to a waiting taxi for an obviously wealthy and distinguished lady.

6

THE PALACE SILENCES
FRANCES WARWICK

The Frank Harris conference at the Ritz is a watershed in the Frances Warwick affair. After that argument in Paris everything changes. The whole story now takes a bizarre twist; new and unexpected personalities are dragged into the intrigue; new moves are initiated, new threats are made. And Frances Warwick herself, who at first was only an anxious woman trying to raise money by any means possible, is transformed into an angry woman recklessly determined to revenge herself on everyone who opposed her plan and even on the man who had tried to help her.

From that moment also it becomes apparent that everyone concerned in the affair was playing a double game. Except, ironically enough, Frank Harris. That man's aims were brutally simple and direct. All he wanted, and he made no bones about it, was to see Edward's letters published in America and to make himself a small fortune.

But everyone else was acting a part, all of them pretending to do one thing but really trying to do another. Lady Warwick certainly was. Still keeping up the pretense that if her demands were not met at once the letters would be handed over to American publishers within a few days, she was actually waiting confidently for the Palace—or some other "interested party"—to hand over the £100,000 she had asked for, and the most bizarre twist in the story was probably what happened later when she suddenly realized that the Palace was trying to get out of paying a penny by resorting to law to keep her quiet. We shall see how Frances, Countess of Warwick, incensed by this, eventually lashed out in fury, extended her "blackmail" threat beyond the Royal Family to the whole gallery of men she had known, and even threatened Arthur du Cros himself!

Du Cros was also playing a double game. But that was imposed upon him by the position he had been steered into as "neutral" intermediary between Lady Warwick and the Palace. While he tried, in all good faith, to save Lady Warwick from financial disaster without letting her disgrace herself, he had at the same time, out of loyalty to King and Country, to work hand-in-glove with courtiers and the King's solicitors, who were determined to defeat and silence her completely by any means in their power.

But the deepest double game of all was that played by the Palace. The King's advisers had only one aim —to keep a Royal scandal secret, whatever happened to Lady Warwick. All the time that they were going through the motions of negotiating amicably with Lady Warwick through Arthur du Cros, allowing him to expend money, time and energy in the process, they were planning an entirely different and drastic course of action, one they had to keep secret even from du Cros until the last possible moment.

We shall see later how the Palace eventually used the full force of the Establishment to remove even from public legal records every trace of the moves they made against Lady Warwick and thus believed that the "Darling Daisy" affair would be buried forever. This surprising fact was revealed when a search of the Public Records Office yielded virtually no details about the "Darling Daisy" affair. But even before that search was made, the documents discovered in Switzerland were sufficient to suggest that Stamfordham and Russell were already making their own plans against Lady Warwick at the very time they accepted du Cros' offer to go to Paris to meet Harris.

Nevertheless, not one word about the Palace's

intentions was uttered by Lord Stamfordham when he met du Cros at Charles Russell's office in Norfolk Street on July 17.

Du Cros had already shown Russell "the rough statement of account" in which Lady Warwick had summarized her debts, and had given the solicitor the ultimatum she had described as the "alternative arrangement." When he went to this second interview with Stamfordham he carried with him a scheme which he felt might clear up the whole business. He suggested a financial agreement by which Lady Warwick's debts could be taken over by "interested parties" in return for her handing over to those parties all rights in the letters and in her memoirs.

By this time even du Cros was finding his original knight-errant enthusiasm waning. He hoped his suggestion would be accepted and his part in the affair would be finished, so, after telling Stamfordham what had happened in Paris, he put the above suggestion to Stamfordham and then asked outright "whether it was necessary that I should continue these communications with Lady Warwick." Obviously he now felt he had done enough: he had performed a loyal duty by warning the Palace and investigating the situation; now it was up to them.

But the Palace still needed him. One thing that was worrying them was the fear that before they

could get their own secret plan into action Lady
Warwick might make some irrevocable move with the
letters. She might, for instance, send them out of the
country. Or, and this fear was even greater, Frank
Harris might do so. Did du Cros know, they asked
anxiously, where the letters were at the moment? He
took it for granted, he said, that they were in her
possession. Only the day before she had sent a
telegram asking for the return of the letters she had
lent to him and had sent someone to his office to collect the envelope. But the King's advisers were less
sanguine than du Cros. One of them—du Cros does
not say whether it was Stamfordham or Russell—
asked if he were sure that she had the other letters.
Was it possible that Frank Harris might have them?
Could du Cros find out?

He promised to do this. When he tried to get in
touch with Lady Warwick in town, he found that
she was on her way back to Easton. He hurried to
Liverpool Street Station and arrived just in time to
have a word with her before her train left. He asked
her, he records, "whether Mr. Frank Harris had
been entrusted with copies or photographs of the
letters," and she replied that he had not. "Put that
in writing to me, please," he called as the train
pulled out. She did. She wrote to him. It was a revealing and important letter, so much so that du
Cros had an extract copied out and sent round to
Russell's office. The King's solicitor also recognized

the importance of the letter and he quoted it in the affidavit he made ten days later.

This particular letter was not among the cache of "Darling Daisy" documents unearthed in Switzerland. Almost certainly Russell asked du Cros to send it to him when he was preparing his affidavit and kept it as evidence to be produced in court. If so, it went up in flames a year later when, as we shall see, the Palace, in an attempt to stamp the "Darling Daisy" scandal into secrecy forever, succeeded in getting a Judge's order that "documents contained in a sealed envelope . . . forthwith to be destroyed."

However, the vital passage quoted by Russell in his affidavit shows why he attached so much importance to it. Apart from her assurance that Edward's letters were not in Harris' possession—and never had been, having merely been shown to him by the mysterious never-named emissary, someone of great rank and note in the world—Frances Warwick's letter was also valuable to Russell because he recognized it as a frank avowal that she considered herself the prime mover in the plan to publish Edward's letters and had employed Frank Harris merely as ghost and agent. To put du Cros and the Palace at ease, she also mentioned that she had made suitable arrangements for the security of the letters in the event of her death.

This somewhat relieved the Palace, and perhaps

Stamfordham could now put the Lady Warwick file aside for a day or two while he attended to the far more somber worries crowding in on his King. On the very day Stamfordham had been meeting du Cros in Russell's office King George had given an audience to the Prime Minister, Asquith, and it had been agreed that the King should summon a conference of government and Irish leaders to discuss moves to avert civil war. The Labour Party had attacked this move with a resolution protesting the "undue interference of the Crown" in matters of national policy, and it was now Stamfordham's task to maintain hourly contact between King, advisers and government during a precarious and sensitive period of political maneuvers.

Meanwhile du Cros was allowed to keep up the pretense of negotiations with the Countess of Warwick. After he had received that letter from Easton, Russell agreed that it might be worth while discussing with her the plan of settlement du Cros had outlined to Stamfordham. Dutifully he went down to Easton to put it before her. Let him tell it in his own words:

> I visited Lady Warwick at Easton to ascertain whether she would prove the *bona fides* of her statement by consenting to an arrangement, if any, taking the following form:—
>
> All rights in her Memoirs to be sold outright,

part payment to be made by taking up judgments and bills outstanding against her by settlement of certain accounts. These bills and accounts to be kept alive and held as security for the observance of the agreement, and to become operative against her if the agreement were not observed.

It was a neat way of tying Lady Warwick up, and not, in the circumstances, unduly harsh. Instead of completely freeing her from debt and thus making it possible that at some time later she might come back with the threat of publishing her memoirs, her debts were to be taken over and "kept alive" as a threat constantly hanging over her head so that she would not be able to play the game again. Frances Warwick, reports du Cros, assented to the principle of this arrangement, and on the following day, July 20 —the same day that the Dowager Queen Alexandra, widow of Frances Warwick's Royal lover, announced that she was to leave for Denmark on holiday—du Cros gave the news of Lady Warwick's assent to Russell. After doing that, he no doubt felt that everything was going in good order and the whole affair might soon be settled.

Not so Lady Warwick, however. Having "assented in principle" to du Cros' suggestion, she suddenly changed her tactics and allowed a direct attack to be initiated—an attack which demanded

the immediate payment of £100,000 "or else." What
caused this sudden change? A day later it was
revealed that Harris had sent her a telegram urging
her not to "haggle" any more. But was there something else? Had she suddenly become suspicious of
the Palace's professed intentions? Had some rumor
of what was going on behind the scenes been "leaked"
in her direction? Or had another "adviser"—the new
personage who now suddenly appeared on the scene
—told her to press hard and work quickly?

This new character recruited to the negotiations
was Mr. Bruce Logan, a former Army captain who
had at one time been stationed with the 66th Division
at Colchester and was now combining his business as
"loan broker" in offices at 180 Piccadilly with a
reputation as a genial man-about-town who mixed
easily with the wealthy and the aristocratic in London's social life. He knew Lady Warwick intimately
and at one time had lived with his wife at The
Cottage, a small house on her Easton Lodge estate.

When tracing persons who had been involved in
the Lady Warwick affair, I met Mr. Bruce Logan
at the lovely rambling cottage in the high street of a
Hertfordshire town in which he was spending his
retirement. It may be that he considered the services
he performed to help Frances Warwick in her battle with the Palace were too intimate to be disclosed
in exact detail, for he expressed his regret that he
could not now remember just what had happened at

the time. Though he could not refrain from recalling, with something of a sigh and with as much
fervor as an elderly man could say such a thing in
the presence of his wife, "Yes, Frances Warwick
was indeed a beautiful woman. Very beautiful and
very fascinating." He himself, a tall man of un-
mistakable military bearing, could still be recognized as a man who must in 1914 have had the
masculine presence and good looks that always appealed to Lady Warwick.*

However, despite Mr. Logan's inability to remember or his natural reluctance to disclose secrets, the
part he played in helping Lady Warwick to tighten
the screw on the Palace is amply described in du
Cros' patient notes, in Charles Russell's affidavit and
in information collected from other sources.

Arthur du Cros first realized that Frances Warwick had recruited yet another "intermediary" when
Bruce Logan called on him at his office in Regent
Street on Tuesday, July 21, 1914. The appearance
of Mr. Logan was a disturbing development, both
for Arthur du Cros and for the Palace. But that
July 21 was, in any case, a disturbing day for
everyone. The Conference on Irish Affairs, summoned to Buckingham Palace by King George, had
begun its deliberations, and the King had welcomed

* It is a matter of great regret to me that this genial
survivor of the "Darling Daisy" affair, who expressed his
eagerness to see my version of the story and his part in it in
print, did not live to do so.

the political leaders with a speech in which he said, "The cry of civil war is on the lips of the most responsible of my people." Incidentally, on that same day a collection of Royal letters was sold at Sotheby's for the tiny sum of £79. But those letters were Queen Victoria's and could hardly be expected to have the inflammatory interest of the letters Lady Warwick claimed to have in her secure possession.

When he called on du Cros, Bruce Logan carried with him a letter from Lady Warwick stating that she had now deputed Mr. Logan to act on her behalf as her "business adviser" in all further negotiations regarding the letters. In this letter, du Cros says, she repeated "that she had only one object to serve, which was to obtain freedom from her liabilities, and, subject to this, Mr Logan could deal with the matter."

Bruce Logan was a businessman and he took a firmer and crisper line than Lady Warwick had dared to take. He stated bluntly that if "Mr. du Cros' *friends*" wanted to buy the letters "they had better be quick," for other negotiations were in progress. Harris, he went on, had wired from Paris giving instructions "not to haggle any more." Taking an even stronger line, Bruce Logan told du Cros that it was no good his "friends" trying to impose any conditions at all on their proposed purchase of the letters. Those "friends" must understand that Lady Warwick and Harris were not at all anxious to sell the letters in any case, so they certainly would not agree to conditions. His parting shot showed the temper the negotiations had assumed now that a businessman had come into them: nobody could buy the letters merely by taking over Lady Warwick's debts. They must be bought without any conditions. And payment must be made "*in cash.*"

Immediately after Bruce Logan left Regent Street, du Cros hurried to see Russell at Norfolk Street and tell him about this new turn in the affair. So far as he could understand, he said, Lady Warwick was not prepared to discuss the matter with him personally any more. Mr. Bruce Logan had apparently become her only accepted intermediary.

This must indeed have been bad news for Russell. The Palace had lost their "neutral" intermediary, and now everything this loyal and zealous servant had told them about the safety of the letters was thrown into doubt. With his close communication with Lady Warwick cut off, they could no longer feel assured that the letters were still securely in her possession. Their doubts and alarm were increased when yet another character appeared on the scene.

This was none other than Clarence Hatry, a man whose name fifteen years later resounded through the world as the perpetrator of a swindle on the Stock Exchange that left in its wake a litter of commercial failures and bankruptcies. The "Darling Daisy" story has shown us how small and incestuously interwoven is the world of high society. The world of finance, it seems, is just as small, for this same Clarence Hatry who in 1914 intruded into the negotiations being conducted by Arthur du Cros was in 1929 to wreck du Cros' financial empire. The banker Sir Edward Beddington-Behrens, publishing recently some of the secrets of the 1929 "Hatry crash," tells how Hatry on one occasion showed du Cros "a long telegram purporting to come from the United States Steel Company saying they would provide a very large sum to finance Hatry's steel operation. On receipt of this telegram du Cros' firm, the Parent Trust, advanced further large amounts to Hatry. Mr Guy, the Parent Trust's managing director, arrived in New York the day of the Hatry crash to find that the telegram was a complete fraud." Sir Edward claims that in 1929 du Cros was "impoverished to the tune of several £ millions" by this same Clarence Hatry who in 1914 first came into du Cros' life as one of the go-betweens in the "Darling Daisy" affair.

At that time Clarence Hatry was an insurance broker, just beginning his business career in London. Even in those days he was showing a talent for quick-thinking and imaginative methods in manipulating money. He was in partnership with Bruce Logan and, like him, was acting as a "loan broker." Hatry had brought to the business a new technique which had already become a considerable success. His association with Bruce Logan and his contacts in London's social life had brought to his office many clients —among them a lot of young officers and similar offspring of good family who, as always with such people, often wanted to get hold of some ready money. But these young men-about-town repeatedly found themselves unable to get a loan on their future expectations because whenever they tried to do so they were asked to provide *two* guarantors for the debt. Each of these young men had little difficulty in finding *one* guarantor among their relations or close friends, but most of them were unable to find a second. Clarence Hatry hit upon an ingenious and simple method of overcoming this handicap. His method was to link up any two borrowers who could find only one guarantor and then, by a series of tactful interviews and exchanges, to "marry" each young man's separate guarantor, thus providing each client with the necessary two. It is one of those simple devices which, after it is explained, make one wonder why no one has thought of it before, but until Clarence Hatry got busy on it no one had done it before, at least not on so extensive a scale as Hatry, and by 1914 he was handling an ever increasing amount of business. So much so that he was reputed to be earning at least £5,000 a year—a great deal of money at that time—by this enterprise alone.

This, then, was the beginning of Clarence Hatry's

spectacular financial career, a career that eventually carried him to the heights of wealth and influence in commerce before the disastrous moment when his astute but not very scrupulous brain thought up a scheme for making a vast Stock Exchange haul overnight to buttress his financial empire. That dangerous enterprise, which, he claimed, he would have been able to conclude profitably within a matter of days, brought down the Hatry companies in ruin, created a nationwide financial crisis and sent him to jail, as well as losing du Cros some of his millions.

Clarence Hatry's involvement in the Lady Warwick affair was a strange one, and the details take the whole affair even further into the realms of Edwardian melodrama. During my researches into the "Darling Daisy" intrigue there came into my hands a remarkable document—a few folios of typescript from an autobiography Clarence Hatry began writing in the 1950's and never completed. These pages tell his story of his contact with Edward's love letters, and it is worth while giving his version as he wrote it. Here it is:

Although my clients usually had two attributes in common—membership of what in those days was still a clearly defined aristocracy, and an urgent desire for money to replace the inheritances that had been recklessly squandered—individually, they often differed consid-

erably. One of the most unusual was the then
Countess of Warwick.

She had been a noted beauty during the last
years of Queen Victoria's reign and into the
palmy Edwardian era, a favourite in Court
circles and an intimate friend of the late King
Edward himself. Aged fifty-three when I first
met her, she still bore traces of that loveliness
that had made many a noble pulse beat faster.
It was sad and ironic, I thought at the time,
that beauty and wealth, the possessions that had
been spent so heedlessly through days and
nights of enjoyment, should prove to be so
impermanent. The Countess needed to raise ten
thousand pounds.

One of her guarantors was Arthur du Cros,
Chairman of the Dunlop Rubber Company. As
I recall the details, we had no difficulty in
arranging the necessary insurance for Lady
Warwick and, once the formalities were com-
plete, I considered the matter closed.

A colleague of mine then, as I have already
mentioned, was Bruce Logan. Apart from his
noted athletic prowess, he was a handsome and
chivalrous young man. Through the business
association he became quite friendly with Lady
Warwick. One afternoon he walked into our
office at 180 Piccadilly carrying a bulky envelope. He had been having tea, he told me, with

Lady W who had entrusted some valuable documents to his safe keeping. He asked my permission to put them in my office safe for the time being. I naturally agreed and took the envelope from him. Without even glancing at its contents, I put it into the safe, then locked the door. Within a few minutes I had completely forgotten the trivial incident.

The next day the uneasy suspicion grew on me that I was being followed wherever I went. In my journeys from home to office and from office to various business and social appointments, I began to notice that a certain stolid-looking man in a bowler hat always contrived to be strolling in a leisurely and at the same time curiously deliberate manner a few paces behind me. At first I laughed the thought away as a figment of an over-active imagination. But he was always there. Coincidences can happen but this burly figure was recurring too often to be a coincidence. Stranger still, I never found him actually looking in my direction. If I turned round suddenly and stared straight at him, his gaze was always directed elsewhere. Although I had done nothing to warrant having my footsteps dogged in this way, I became somewhat uneasy.

That same morning Bruce Logan entered the office. His usual healthy flush had given way to pallor and he seemed to be worried about something. I went straight to the point.

"Bruce," I demanded, "do you think you're being followed?"

He gave a visible start. "It's odd you should say that. Yes, I'm certain someone is following me. Why do you ask? Are *you* being followed, too?"

For answer I went over to the window and looked discreetly down the street. There, standing near a lamp-post, apparently absorbed in a newspaper, was my stolid companion with the bowler hat. Bruce Logan joined me at the window and peeped out. Clutching my arm with one hand, he pointed with the other. "Look," he said. I looked. A few yards up the street, shifting his weight from one foot to the other and to all intents and purposes studying the local architecture, was another bowler-hatted character who might have been the twin of my stalker. Neither of them took the slightest notice of the other.

For several days the pursuit continued. I became almost attached to my unsolicited attendant. On one occasion after crossing a busy street and finding that he had been cut off on the other side by the traffic, I paused to allow him time to catch up with me. My conscience was clear and if someone was foolish enough to employ an ex-policeman (for such he obviously was) to keep track of my movements, there was no reason for me to get angry with the dutiful employee.

Some days later one morning there came a knock on the office door. My secretary came in to tell me that one of the partners in the well known firm of lawyers, Messrs Russell, wished to see Bruce Logan and me. Wondering what it could be about, I asked her to show him in. A grave-faced man entered and presented his professional card. I hardly glanced at it when he produced a more formidable document. It was an injunction. I recognised the impressive list of names at once. It was the style that the Monarch adopted for his private business.

Trying to disguise my nervousness, I read through the injunction. It was made out against Bruce Logan and myself and it enjoined us not to part with certain documents now in our possession nor to cause these same documents to be published either severally or jointly. The applicant, in whose Royal name the injunction had been made out, claimed copyright in the papers now residing in my safe, as they had been written by his father and were thus legally the property of the writer or rather, since the writer was now dead, the property of his successor, the then King.

To say that I was dumbfounded would be an understatement. As soon as my visitor had left, I sent word for Bruce Logan to call on me at once. When he arrived, I told him briefly what had happened and then demanded to know what all this bother was about. He told me and, as he spoke, I could feel the sweat breaking out on my forehead.

It turned out that the letters which I had thrust airily into my safe without so much as glancing at them were private correspondence which the late Edward VII had written to his good friend, the Countess of Warwick, over a period of several years. They were the kind of intimate, careless note that old friends drop each other, what in modern jargon might be called "off the record" letters. They apparently contained slighting references to the Kaiser, whom Edward cordially disliked, uncomplimentary remarks about certain Cabinet Ministers and smoking-room stories that the King had heard late at night when the port had circulated freely. The Countess had come across this bundle of letters when looking through her private papers. Somehow a publisher had come to realise their existence.

The publisher, realising that here might be the "scoop" of the century, had made a very handsome offer to Lady Warwick for the publi-

cation rights. But what might be a best seller
for a publisher could be a deadly threat to the
Monarchy. Publication of these private letters,
tossed off in unthinking moments, could be a
constitutional bombshell that would certainly
precipitate a General Election and might do the
Royal Family untold harm. For the general
public to know that the late King had discussed
leading personalities and even State secrets,
however innocently, with an old and trusted
friend who had no right to be acquainted with
such details could shake the Throne itself.

Lady Warwick had, I believed, confided her
predicament to members of the Royal Household. She needed money badly and here was a
golden opportunity of obtaining plenty. On the
other hand she suspected the dangers to herself
and others of open publication. What should be
done?

King George V acted with characteristic vig-
our. Having discovered the whereabouts of the
letters, he acted in his capacity as a private
citizen and had the injunction sworn against
Bruce Logan and myself, the unconscious and
entirely innocent possessors for the time being
of the deadly documents. When I heard all this,
I felt rather like the man who accepts a lift in a
lorry along a bumpy country road and then
discovers, half way along the route, that the

lorry is loaded with nitro-glycerine which is liable to explode at the slightest jar.

Delicate negotiations continued for several weeks. The King was naturally reluctant to press his claims to the letters as far as the courts where publicity which he wished to avoid at all costs was inevitable. The Countess was equally reluctant to give away property of potential great value at a time when she was not too well off. Deadlock was reached and all the time those letters resided in my safe, tucked away in a dark corner. I began to realise what it must be like to keep a cobra as a pet.

At last a solution, acceptable to both parties, was reached. Arthur du Cros, already mentioned as one of the Countess's guarantors, proposed that he should purchase the letters from her for an agreed sum, at the same time giving his solemn word that he would personally destroy the letters as soon as they were in his possession. It was the perfect British compromise. I cannot describe the feeling of relief that surged over me when the letters were finally removed from my safe. Not long afterwards Arthur du Cros received a baronetcy. It was a well deserved honour.

This anecdote had an odd sequel some seven or eight years later. A colleague on one of my company boards, Sir Douglas Dawson, who had been an Equerry to the King, told me that when my name had been put forward for a certain honour, His Majesty was scrutinising the letters patent before signing them. He turned to his Equerry and said, "Hatry? Hatry? Isn't that the little so-and-so we had trouble with over my father's letters?" My friend was able to assure him that I had been an innocent party to the matter and had acted with propriety throughout. With his hearty sailor's laugh, George V dismissed the memory of what might have been almost the biggest Court scandal of the twentieth century.

I confess that when I first heard Clarence Hatry's allegation that the Palace had put private detectives on his trail I found it hard to believe. I could not credit that the Royal Family, or, rather, solicitors acting for them, would employ such methods. But, as we shall learn later, this was actually done.

It appears that Frances Warwick herself had become frightened that some attempt, legal or otherwise, might be made to get the letters out of her possession. This apparently was why she had given them to her new ally, Bruce Logan, and asked him to put them in some safe place. We also know that during the period when the King's solicitors were preparing their final blow against Frances Warwick the one thing causing intense disquiet in Russell's office was the fear that the letters might be taken out of the country.

Bruce Logan knew he had to act forcefully and quickly on Frances Warwick's behalf. Only one day after he had first called at du Cros' office he called again. This time he played an even stronger card. He now told du Cros that "they"—by which he meant himself, Lady Warwick and, apparently, Harris— were now even less anxious than they had been twenty-four hours before to sell the letters. "Either to you," he said bluntly to du Cros—and out it came boldly—"or to *any member of the Royal Family.*" He explained the reason for this increased reluctance to sell. "The letters were about to be sold to '*a group*' who might put up a larger figure, namely £150,000, for them and there were several Americans in the deal."

These negotiations, Bruce Logan further warned du Cros, "would probably be closed on the following day." Full of anxiety, du Cros informed Russell of this new development, and Russell—still anxious to use du Cros as the intermediary—asked du Cros to keep Bruce Logan at bay. So next day, July 23, du Cros telephoned Logan and begged him not to "finally close anything without first informing me." According to du Cros, Logan agreed to this, and du Cros, still hoping that he could use his own influence with Lady Warwick to avert disaster, decided to appeal directly to her over Logan's head. He made an appointment to meet her and discuss the new situation.

But a day later du Cros had devastating news. This is how he tells it:

> On the 24th, however, I received a definite message from Mr Logan to the effect that the negotiations to which he had referred had been concluded, that a deposit had been paid to Lady Warwick and that the matter was, therefore, at an end so far as I was concerned.

Immediately du Cros telephoned St. James's Palace to give this news to Stamfordham, and, not being able to get in touch with Russell by telephone, sent him a wire.

> HAVE JUST BEEN INFORMED DEFINITELY NEGOTIATIONS REFERRED TO OUR INTERVIEW THURSDAY HAVE NOW BEEN COMPLETED AND MATTER CLOSED FEAR THEREFORE I CAN DO NOTHING MORE FOR YOU BUT WILL ENDEAVOUR OBTAIN PARTICULARS FOR YOUR INFORMATION SHALL BE IN TOWN MONDAY AFTERNOON I HAVE TELEPHONED LORD S.

Despite this news, neither Stamfordham nor Russell revealed the fact that their plans to silence Lady Warwick were now well under way, and du Cros tried to get to Lady Warwick and talk the matter over. He still hoped that she might accept his advice, and this hope was fortified when she agreed to a meeting and fixed an appointment. That hope was short-lived. She had also made an appointment with her lawyer, Sir Henry Paget-Cooke, but then telephoned Sir Henry, "cancelling the appointment because she had now completed her arrangements" and asking Sir Henry to inform Mr. du Cros to that effect.

Thus ended July 24. It seemed to du Cros a day of disaster. It was also, on a grander scale, a day of disaster for Europe. It was the day Austria served the ultimatum on Serbia following the Sarajevo assassination, and the British Foreign Secretary, Sir Edward Grey, was requesting the audience with King George at which he would inform his sovereign of the imminent possibility of war in Europe. It was even being rumored that the King might abandon his plans to attend the Cowes Regatta.

Du Cros continued his efforts to see Lady Warwick, sending telegrams and telephone messages suggesting an interview to talk things over, and at last she agreed to see him at Eaton Square on the 25th. But on the morning of the 25th—the morning when Grey was at Buckingham Palace telling his grave news and the Admiralty had decided to cancel Navy leave and order the British Fleet to "stand by"—du Cros received a message which made it appear that now nothing could stop the march of events. The message awaiting him on his office desk said:

> *Lady Warwick phones she will not be keeping*
> *her appointment with you today as she is going*
> *to Easton by the 11.40. The matter has now*
> *passed out of her hands and she has completed*
> *her arrangements and there is no more to be*
> *said. Please tell Mr du Cros that I have now*
> *completed arrangements elsewhere and there is*
> *no further purpose to be served.*

This seemed final enough, but even so du Cros continued his efforts. He turned to Bruce Logan, but was not able to contact him for two days.

On the 27th July I telephoned Mr Logan to ask him whether the negotiations he had concluded would necessarily result in the publication of the letters. He informed me the transaction was a private one with a private individual and that the letters had not been purchased for publication and would *not* be published.

That, at any rate, was a bit better, and with some feeling of relief du Cros reported it to Charles Russell. The King's solicitor accepted the news without comment. He was now confident that within a matter of hours neither Lady Warwick's threats to publish nor Bruce Logan's assurances that no publication was planned would any longer matter. Lady Warwick was due to be silenced completely.

Frances Warwick, however, was apparently not quite confident about the outcome of her own negotiations. Something or other that had happened in the last day or so made her want to resume contact with du Cros, and on July 28 she unexpectedly sent a message to Regent Street asking to see him. Du Cros dutifully reported this change to Russell. The King's solicitor advised that it might be as well to see what the lady wanted, and du Cros made an appointment for that afternoon.

What had happened to make Frances Warwick change tack and agree to see du Cros again? There is a hint of the reason in du Cros' notes of this interview. He does not himself seem to have been aware how important that reason was. Certainly he does not draw special attention to that part of her conversation, but it is significant. At that interview Frances Warwick revealed that she was now experiencing pressure from another source. Her own family—her husband, or her sons, or some other aristocratic relatives—were now urging her not to disgrace herself and, indirectly, the family name. Here, however, is du Cros' summary of the conversation:

Lady Warwick then informed me that her relatives had intervened very strongly in the matter but her determination had not been altered, and that in fact it was practically too late to make any alteration as she had received a monetary deposit in respect of an agreement to hand over the letters which although not actually signed would be confirmed from America in the course of a few days.

Once again we are faced with the question we asked at the very beginning of this story when Lady Warwick first revealed to du Cros that she was intending to publish the letters: If an agreement really *had* been made, what purpose was served by telling du Cros at all? The answer is the same answer we arrived at on that first occasion. Frances Warwick was still anxious not to do anything so disgraceful as publishing the letters or selling them in America. She wanted to do nothing more disgraceful, in fact, than quietly and privately extort money from the Royal Family. Her statement that it was *"practically* too late" was a hint that if the Royal Family or any interested party in Britain was prepared to pay up, then even at this late stage the agreement with the American buyers—"not actually signed"—could be upset.

It seems that at this critical juncture du Cros was getting weary of the whole business. Perhaps he was beginning to think that the matter was out of his hands for good and that he could do nothing more. The Palace, however, had other views, and on July 29 Charles Russell suddenly became desperately anxious to see du Cros. Early that morning he sent a telegram to Canons, du Cros' Edgware home, asking him to ring him at once at his Kensington home, where he would be until 9.40 a.m. This telegram reached Canons too late to catch the energetic early-rising du Cros, but his wife telephoned the message to the Regent Street office. The message did not catch him, however, for du Cros had business in the City that day, so another urgent message came later to Regent Street asking du Cros to call on Russell that afternoon.

There is no evidence in the documents that this appointment was kept. Perhaps, at last, du Cros was attending too energetically to his own affairs to be free for any more of these Lady Warwick interviews. But among the documents is the telegram Charles Russell sent to Arthur du Cros at the House of Commons on the afternoon of July 30 asking him to ring up the King's solicitor immediately. July 30, 1914, however, was a day when any loyal M.P. could hardly be expected to leave the Commons. Fearful and ominous news hovered over the Chamber. Germany had marched violently into the quarrel between Austria and Serbia. Russia and France were talking of war.

So it was not until July 31 that du Cros went to Russell's office. Even to him, so intimately concerned in the Lady Warwick intrigue, the visit must have seemed an anti-climax after what had happened in the Commons. The Prime Minister had informed the

House that Russia was mobilizing and that martial law had been declared in Germany. News was also around that King George had sent a personal telegram to the Czar assuring him of British sympathy and expressing the hope that in this grave moment steps might be taken to avert war. Suddenly, as though awaking from a summer dream, Britain realized that she was on the brink of war and that the Sarajevo assassination had burgeoned into world catastrophe. The King had now definitely canceled his plans to go to Cowes and was instead waiting to receive his Prime Minister in audience.

Despite the clouds of war, however, King George's solicitor, Charles Russell, was that day no doubt in a state of confidence, if not jubilation. Whatever terrors Germany and Austria might be threatening to unleash upon the world and Britain, he had succeeded in rescuing his sovereign from the threats of Frances, Countess of Warwick. One, at least, of the King's enemies had been defeated.

Russell told du Cros the news. There was now, he said, no danger of Lady Warwick publishing the late King Edward's letters. She was completely unable to do so. An injunction against their publication had been applied for in Chambers (i.e., not in open court) and an interlocutory injunction had been granted.

Nothing better illustrates the secrecy in which Stamfordham and Russell worked than the way they handled the injunction. The Cause Book of the King's Bench Division shows that the writ in the action was issued out of the High Court at the Central Office in the Strand at 3.25 p.m. on July 29, 1914, the day after Russell had agreed that du Cros might as well agree to see Lady Warwick again. But it can be assumed that preparations must have been put in hand before that, for the negotiations must have involved comings and goings between Russell and counsel about the form of the writ and affidavit.

The speed with which Charles Russell was able to announce to du Cros that the injunction had been granted suggests that the application was probably made "ex parte"—that is, without any notice being given to the defendants. All that happens in such a case is that, after issue of the writ, the applicants go before the judge armed with an affidavit.

The documents unearthed in Switzerland make it seem that this is what did happen, for we know from du Cros' notes that it was at this interview in Russell's office that the King's solicitor handed an affidavit to du Cros. This document, bound lawyer-fashion in green tape, is a vital document in the "Darling Daisy" affair, because it is the actual affidavit which Charles Russell himself had sworn in his own office two days earlier before a Mr. W. James, Commissioner for Oaths, and from which I have quoted previously in the story. The Central Office from which the writ was issued was in the Strand, only a few steps from the Norfolk Street office of Charles Russell and Co.

Russell's affidavit gives the outline of the Lady Warwick intrigue as seen by him from the day, July 9, when du Cros first came to see him on the matter. It records what du Cros told him then—it even quotes some of Lady Warwick's phrases, such as the one she used in her first letter to du Cros when she warned him that she was preparing a sensational publication. The affidavit also describes the sudden irruption of Mr. Bruce Logan into the affair.

But the most interesting, and indeed amusing, feature of the document is that never once is "dear Edward" mentioned by name. The injunction is sought against the publication of "a great number of private letters of a most confidential character *from the Testator*." The affidavit talks of Lady Warwick giving du Cros "three of the said Testator's letters," and of Mr. Logan telling du Cros that "they were not in the least anxious to dispose of the letters to Mr du Cros' friends or to any member of the Testator's family."

The judge, of course, well knew who that mysterious "Testator" was. In any case, anyone who read the names of the plaintiffs who made the application would know the same. Those plaintiffs, three of them, were listed as "the Right Honourable Sir Dighton Macnaghten Probyn, the Right Honourable the

Viscount Knollys and Colonel Sir Arthur Davidson."

Sir Dighton Probyn, who died in 1924, was in
1914 an extra equerry to King George. He had been
equerry to King Edward and was, after Edward's
death, comptroller to Queen Alexandra's household.
Viscount Knollys was an even more important employee of the Royal Household and even more closely
involved in the private affairs of the Royal Family.
He had been Edward's private secretary for no less
than forty years—for thirty-one years when Edward
was Prince of Wales and nine years when he was
King. He continued in that important office for King
George, serving him as private secretary from 1910
to 1913, and was lord-in-waiting to Queen Alexandra. He died in 1924 also. Sir Arthur Davidson,
who died in 1922, was in 1914 equerry to King
George and lord-in-waiting to Queen Alexandra.

Russell's affidavit also refers to something described as "the exhibit marked 'A.' " This was presented to the judge attached to an affidavit sworn by
Viscount Knollys, and the context in which Russell
mentions this "exhibit" suggests that it was a copy
of one of Edward's letters.

Thus, if the application for the injunction had
been made in open court instead of "in Chambers,"
the truth about the "Testator" would inevitably
have become common knowledge to everyone in Britain. Indeed, everything was in the Palace's favor.

The very date of the application helped them to avoid publicity. The long vacation was just about to begin and no one was paying close attention to what was happening in and around the courts. If an "ex parte" injunction was granted, it would be for a few days only and a hearing would have to take place at which all the parties, plaintiffs and defendants, would have to be present. If there was such a second hearing, it would take place in the early part of the long vacation.

However, the Palace so diligently covered up their tracks that any legal maneuvers they performed have been hidden from history. For instance, no one seems to have entered in the Cause Book of the King's Bench Division any significant details of the action. Apart from recording that a writ was issued, the clerk in charge recorded nothing more except the fact that one of the defendants, a certain Mr. Frank Harris, was in France and therefore had, under rules of court, the longer period of twelve days in which to enter his appearance.

The Russell affidavit, however, reveals as much as we need to know. Most significantly, the first of the defendants named is none other than Mr. Bruce Logan. Since his involvement in the "Darling Daisy" affair was known to the Palace only from about July 21, it can be assumed that he was introduced as a party in the action after that date. By July 29 he must have appeared to Stamfordham

and Russell as the main danger. The other defend-
ants named after him are "the Right Honourable
Frances Evelyn Countess of Warwick, the Right
Honourable Francis Richard Charles Guy Greville
Earl of Warwick and Frank Harris."

How and why is Frances Warwick's husband, the
Earl, suddenly dragged into the affair? Up to now he
has been merely someone in the background, the
husband almost forgotten through the years of
Frances Warwick's love affairs and never even mentioned by du Cros or anyone else involved in her
negotiations about "dear Edward's" letters. Charles
Russell explains in his affidavit why this shadowy
figure is brought into the light. The last paragraph
reads:

> The Defendant, the Earl of Warwick, resides
> with the Countess at Easton Lodge, Dunmow,
> in the County of Essex, where she has been
> writing her Memoirs for some time past, and I
> verily believe that he is cognisant of the before-
> mentioned matters in which the Countess is
> concerned.

Against this paragraph du Cros tetchily penciled
his firm opinion that the Earl of Warwick knew
nothing at all about the affair.

Anyhow, after that one brief mention in the story
of Frances Warwick's intrigue the Earl sinks into
the background again, a dutiful husband, remaining

—as he seems to have remained throughout his life—
a complaisant bystander, accepting her infidelities,
her ruinous extravagances, her reckless actions. Or at
least suffering them without protest or interference.

What makes Russell's affidavit a fascinating document now is something far more interesting than
anything the solicitor actually said in it. That
something is the penciled scribbling du Cros made on
its margins after Russell had lent him the document
and asked him to use it as a basis for the full
statement du Cros had to make on the part he had
played.

One of the penciled notes is written beside that
part of the affidavit where Russell states that du
Cros had told him "he felt it desirable to go to Paris
to meet Lady Warwick and Frank Harris together."
Du Cros, determined that his own attitude should be
perfectly clear, has written in the margin:
"Throughout, A d. C was pressed to act by Russell
and Stamfordham."

But the most interesting and revealing scribbling
comes later. This is where one finds staggering
confirmation of Clarence Hatry's suspicion that
when he had the letters in his safe he was being
watched and followed by private detectives employed
—incredible though it might seem—by Russell and
the Palace. In his marginal note du Cros says that
when Russell handed him the affidavit the King's
solicitor confessed that when du Cros and Frances

Warwick went to Paris "*detectives travelled both ways and watched all the parties.*"

On the first page of Russell's affidavit Arthur du Cros penciled some comments regarding less important conversations he later had when he was beginning to feel annoyed that his part in the affair was being misrepresented, but on the back fold of the document he has written a surprising comment. This reveals that the Palace was planning to go to even greater lengths than an injunction if Frances Warwick could not be disciplined. This is what he says:

> The passage of the Defence of the Realm Act gave extraordinary powers to the Government and was the weapon which brought about L W's surrender. She and others were threatened with arrest.

This note somewhat confused my inquiries into the affair. One of my interviews was with a solicitor, a partner in one of the most eminent law firms in London, who was closely concerned in Lady Warwick's legal affairs. Legal training and personal caution prevented him from answering many of my questions directly with a definite "yes" or "no," but my reference to du Cros' comment about the Defense of the Realm Act elicited a definite statement. The solicitor misunderstood du Cros' note and said almost impatiently: "The court action was not taken under the Defense of the Realm Act. The injunction against the letters being published was granted on the quite ordinary and inevitable grounds that the letters were copyright."

They were, of course. No one, not Lady Warwick or anyone else, could publish the letters in Britain or in any other country that had been a signatory to the Berne and Berlin Conventions on international copyright. But the important words in that sentence are *"in Britain."* America was different. Because the United States had stood aloof from the international conventions, unless a writer took care to register and establish his rights in the United States nothing could prevent anything he had written being published there. In any case, any American publisher with his hands on these letters would have published first and then prepared to do battle later with any lawyers.

Now we can see why the Palace were so preoccupied about the location of the letters, why they were frightened that perhaps Harris had them with him in Paris and might scuttle across the Atlantic to America with them at any moment. No doubt those detectives who followed du Cros and Lady Warwick back and forth from London to Paris kept a close watch not only on Clarence Hatry's Piccadilly office but also Harris' lodgings in Paris.

However, there was one more legal curb the Palace could put on Frances Warwick which might conceivably prevent her publishing the letters even in Amer-

ica. One clause in the 1911 Copyright Act states
that an injunction against publication of any work
*"will also be granted in the case of an unpublished
work where the owner of the copyright fears that his
right is threatened, or that an unauthorised publication is intended."* This clause, Charles Russell must
have advised Stamfordham, could be directly applied
in the Lady Warwick affair. The owner of the
copyright in Edward's letters was, naturally, his son
and heir, King George V. The King could argue, or
at least his solicitors could argue in the courts on his
behalf, that his right in the letters was being *threatened* and that Lady Warwick's plan to publish them
in America was indeed *unauthorized*. So the judge
seems to have thought when the application for an
injunction was made in Chambers, and the plaintiffs,
Messrs. Probyn, Knollys and Davidson, had an easy
passage in their first legal tussle against defendants
Messrs. Logan and Harris and the Warwicks.

It was understandable that the King and his
solicitors would want this legal action to be quiet and
undetected. Nevertheless, the way they did it illustrates the methods by which, even in a country that
fondly believes the processes of government and law
are beautifully and honestly open to the public eye,
legal processes can be conducted in virtual secrecy
by being steered into a private unreported "hearing
in Chambers." Here it was so. Russell conducted the
process with commendable legal expertise and an im-

portant action of undeniably sensational worldwide interest was quickly fought out behind the scenes without anyone outside the intimate circle of the persons involved ever hearing the merest whisper of the desperate struggle.

Russell's admission that detectives had trailed du Cros to Paris indicates the extreme anxiety Frances Warwick's threats to publish had aroused. Stamfordham and Russell were prepared to do even more than use private detectives: they were prepared even to manipulate legal procedure so that the "Darling Daisy" scandal might never become public knowledge. It will be seen later how they succeeded in smothering the evidence which would, in the normal course of events, have been filed in official legal records. The discovery of the documents in Switzerland has uncovered most of the secrets they tried to keep, yet they performed their hushing-up so cleverly that even to this day it is impossible to discover the one thing one would expect to discover most easily: the basis on which the injunction was claimed. Even the writ itself his disappeared into thin air.

I am indebted to a prominent lawyer who diligently searched public records for any trace of these "secret" injunction proceedings. He believes that the injunction may have been sought under "breach of confidence" rather than "infringement of copyright" because this would prohibit "not only reproduction of the letters but also communication of

their contents, thus sabotaging Lady Warwick's plan
to publish in America, where enforcement of the
Royal copyright would have been difficult if not impossible." This legal adviser continues: "Therefore,
the Palace advisers were being very shrewd in not
pinning their hopes on copyright or at any rate on
copyright alone."

Here is this lawyer's account of his subsequent
search for more traces of the case and his legal diag-
nosis of Russell's affidavit:

It is impossible to discover definite evidence
as to the precise basis of the High Court action
instituted against Bruce Logan and the others.
The Public Record Office were unable to find
any trace of any pleadings in the action, i.e. a
Statement of Claim and/or Defence. Nor were
they able to find any affidavits, though this was
only to be expected having regard to the terms
of the final order in the case which, as you
know, decreed that all affidavits filed in this action be taken off the file of the court and returned to the appropriate solicitors.

The Public Record Office did think at one
stage that a copy of the writ would be available
among the archives which they keep out of
London at Ashridge, Herts., but the officials at
Ashridge were unable to trace one. The writ
would, of course, have told us the basis of the

claim. Accordingly, the precise basis of the claim must be a matter of guesswork, though it is possible to have a pretty shrewd idea of what it was on general principle.

What can be said with almost total certainty is that the claim was *not* a claim for the return of the letters. It had already been decided before the Logan case that the ownership in the paper on which letters are written passes to the recipient. In other words, the Countess of Warwick certainly was entitled to the letters as physical objects. The fact that, as a term of settlement, it was agreed that the letters be handed over to the plaintiffs' solicitors does not cast any doubt on this because in a settlement the parties are free to make whatever terms they can agree upon.

The affidavit of Charles Russell sheds practically no light on the nature of the claim. His affidavit is solely concerned with events from the date on which Arthur du Cros first called on him. However, his was not the only affidavit, as appears from Paragraph 2 of Russell's affidavit. There he refers to the affidavit of Viscount Knollys. Incidentally, it can be observed in passing that it would appear from the reference in question that the identity of the Testator (the late King Edward VII) was only disclosed in an exhibit to the Viscount's affidavit.

This shows that the Palace's advisers were being very cunning in that exhibits are not normally left with the court but returned immediately after use. Even if ultimately the court had not ordered the affidavits to be removed, the absence of the exhibit from the Public Records would have prevented the ordinary enquirer from knowing of King Edward's involvement. Only someone with inside knowledge of who the plaintiffs were would be put on enquiry.

It can be guessed that the affidavit of Viscount Knollys said inter alia that the letters had been written by the Testator mentioned in the exhibit and were accordingly the Testator's copyright and that neither the Testator nor his personal representatives had ever given any consent to their publication. Further, the affidavit will almost certainly have said that the letters were written in confidence. *In short, the claim would, therefore, almost certainly have been based on alleged breach of copyright and alleged breach of confidence.* And it may be expected that the Palace's advisers had very much in mind the case of Prince Albert v. Strange, decided in 1849. This was a case in which the Prince Consort of Queen Victoria obtained an injunction against a man called Strange who was about to put on an exhibition of etchings done by Queen Victoria and Prince Albert accompanied by a descriptive catalogue.

So much for the court battle. But what about du Cros' reference to the Defense of the Realm Act— the familiar "Dora" which, on the outbreak of war, was brought into full force to discipline a whole nation facing the threat of war? At first glance one would think that du Cros was becoming somewhat overheated and dramatizing the case out of all proportion. But he had a point. When du Cros refers to that Act as the "weapon which brought about L[ady] W[arwick]'s surrender," he is not, of course, referring to the injunction, as the solicitor I interviewed thought he was. The point du Cros was making lies in the second sentence of that note scribbled on the affidavit. He claims that under the "extraordinary powers" of the Defense of the Realm Act Lady Warwick and others were in danger of arrest. And indeed that is true enough. On August 4, only four days after Russell's affidavit had been thrust into du Cros' hand, Britain declared war on Germany. The nation was now on a military footing, and any person who did anything at all that could conceivably be considered treasonable or even in the smallest way deleterious to the nation's war effort could be summarily arrested. How easy indeed it would be to say that Lady Warwick's threat to publish the letters of the King who had been her lover was an attempt to denigrate the Royal Family, cast odium on the Monarchy and thus automatically, inevitably, discredit the rightful rulers of Britain and play into the hands of Britain's enemies. So we must accept du Cros' statement—probably founded on information obtained from Charles Russell or elsewhere—that Lady Warwick was in danger of arrest. In fact, it is not beyond the bounds of probability that Lady Warwick only narrowly escaped adding a spell in the Tower to the long record of outrageous incidents and changes of fortune for which her life is notable.

Even so, Lady Warwick refused to be silenced. That reckless and tempestuous lady was not going to admit defeat, neither to a judge in Chambers nor even to the full might and majesty of the Defense of the Realm Act, and in November, three months later, she marched in on du Cros again. The way she did so was almost like the beginning of the whole saga all over again. She had not yet paid the interest due on the du Cros loan, and once again his lawyer, Mr. Purchase, had been making demands for settlement. So, just as she had done in the same circumstances in June, she sent on November 19, 1914, a message to du Cros saying that she wished to see him on a matter of importance.

He saw her that same day and was staggered to discover that Frances Warwick was now on another tack. She could not publish Edward's letters. All right. In that case, she had something even more damning that she could publish. Having said that, she handed him some typescript. She did not give him the opportunity of reading it in her presence because she was in full spate of vehemence, but before the interview ended she had told him enough to disquiet him gravely.

She said she would leave the typescript with him to read later, and meanwhile she played the old game of flattery. She told du Cros that he, as a clever businessman, would, by reading between the lines, recognize its potential value. Here is how du Cros reports her description of this new piece of writing:

> She told me it was a specimen chapter from her memoirs, written by Mr F Harris, and that she had written another dealing with the episode of Mr X's letters (King Edward VII's) and had held up to ridicule the people concerned in that matter and their attempts to coerce her.

Her intention was plain. Balked in her attempt to publish the letters, she was going to do something which, so far as the Palace was concerned, could be even worse. She was going to tell the story that I have told in these pages, the full story of the intrigue conducted by the Palace.

As she had done before, she begged, with her pose of sweet ingenuousness, that du Cros, as a friend and clever businessman, would give her advice. But she accompanied this request with a threat, one that struck deep at du Cros. Perhaps those beautiful dark-blue eyes were smiling charmingly when she delivered the blow, but it hit du Cros no less hard. Blandly she told him that she had also heard stories about du Cros himself which laid him open to criticism in his private and business life.

There it was. The lioness at bay. She was determined to raise money by any possible means. She said as much. She said that she positively must get out of her financial difficulties somehow. So she was now prepared to turn even on the man who had tried to help her. Even over him she would dangle the threat of blackmail.

Whatever Arthur du Cros' family or business secrets might have been, the threat seems to have disturbed him hugely. Certainly he seems to have crumbled in the face of it. So much so that he cast around for some way of placating her, trying to think up some other way in which she might earn money and thus avert her blackmail threats. Eventually he grabbed at an idea. What he proposed seems so ludicrous, so unimaginably "cloak and dagger" and incredible, that if it had been reported to me by anyone else I should have discounted it and shoved it aside as too improbable to put into print. But here it lies before me in du Cros' own handwriting. I cannot do better than present it just as he wrote it.

I suggested as an alternative she should by her influence assist in obtaining contracts for war material from the French, Belgian and Russian Governments. This would enable her to make money in a legitimate way. I arranged to introduce her to a firm of general merchants who could utilise her services.

Fantastic! Of all the incidents reported in this story, that certainly is the most fantastic. That anyone could even think of Frances, Countess of Warwick, going into the arms business, let alone seriously suggest it, seems beyond sanity. But perhaps the suggestion is in tune with the general hysteria and melodrama affecting all walks of life in Britain during those early months of the Great War.

In fact, Lady Warwick herself seems to have accepted the suggestion seriously. At least, she promised to call at du Cros' office the following day to arrange to meet one of the partners of this firm. But perhaps she actually went away laughing at the thought that she had met anyone so palpably ingenuous and compliant as dear Arthur du Cros, and on leaving she did not fail to remind him that when she came back she would collect the typescript she had given him and expect to have his advice about it.

As soon as she had gone du Cros read the typescript. Having done so, he was even more distressed.

I found it to be a chapter dealing with Mr Astor. It was very severe in its terms and held him up to public odium both as regards his public and private life.

Mr. Waldorf Astor, then M.P. for Plymouth, had been one of King Edward's favorite millionaires. His wife was later to become world-famous as Nancy, Lady Astor. His stately home, Cliveden, at Taplow in Buckinghamshire, was also to become famous as the supposed meetingplace of the "Cliveden Set," a gathering of notables who became every bit as talked about as Edward's Marlborough House Set, though for different reasons. The group gathered around Cliveden were renowned not so much for luxurious life as for the almost sinister influence they had on government and foreign policy during the growth of Facism and Nazism on the Continent.

Later still, only a few years ago, the Astor home of Cliveden became even more talked about as the scene of those bathing-pool frolics which ended in yet another public scandal, the Profumo affair, and even yet Cliveden has not entirely lived down the notoriety it earned in that unsavory episode.

When du Cros read Lady Warwick's frank revelations about Mr. Astor he was uneasy at the thought of what that same hand might write about him. He says so in his notes.

(*237*)

I formed the opinion that L W's intention was to convey to me that if my Solicitor pressed her for the money due that she would retaliate by writing me up in her memoirs.

So when she called on him the following day he "earnestly advised her not to be persuaded by Harris or anyone else into publishing attacks on individuals which would react against her own character and entail reprisals from them."

To his great relief, she accepted this advice. Obviously, she felt that she had made her point. She had demonstrated to du Cros that if his solicitor continued dunning her for his miserable money she could wreak her revenge. She promised to instruct Harris, who was now in America, not to proceed on the lines she had threatened. Then, even more strange, she agreed to meet the partner of the firm of general merchants and actually went into the armaments business. It is hard to believe that Frances, Socialist Countess of Warwick, should engage in any such enterprise when quite a few of the friends she had made in the Socialist Party were being hustled off to prison, or were in danger of being hustled off, for campaigning against the war effort and for their refusal to do military service. But du Cros reports quite clearly that she did attempt it, that she embarked upon the attempt to obtain business contracts.

His notes refer to two letters he received from her after this interview. Perhaps these were letters about armament contracts, and he may have considered them too "top secret" to be included with his growing file about Lady Warwick and her supposed memoirs. Whatever the reason, they are, unfortunately, not included in the documents in my possession, but his records do show that she came to see him two months later, on January 18, 1915, and "told me what had occurred about war contracts." What she told him he does not say. Perhaps that also was "top secret."

In any case, she had something of more personal importance and urgency to report. She had received a letter from that eminent law firm to which I have referred above. According to du Cros, this letter was one "asking for instructions to retain Sir E. Carson on her behalf under circumstances not explained."

Lady Warwick did not understand the reason for the letter and I advised her to see them and ask for an explanation.

During the interview she also told him that, owing to the war, an income of £6,000 a year that she had been receiving from Belgium had stopped, and that consequently she and her family were in deeper financial distress than ever. Added to that, there were actions pending for the bankruptcy of her husband, Lord Warwick. Du Cros asked her to get her husband's agent at Warwick Castle, Godfrey Payton, to confer with him. It appears that du Cros, despite Frances Warwick's assurance that she would not write attacks on private personages, including Arthur du Cros, was still trying to keep her sweet. Certainly in the arrangement he now made with Payton he retreated completely from his original demand that he must have the dividends due to him. He arranged that the creditors threatening bankruptcy should be stalled off with payments out of these dividends, and also agreed to "the release of dividends amounting to £100 per week for L W's necessities."

Meanwhile Frances Warwick went to see the solicitors who had written to her. She came back to du Cros with surprising news. They had offered her a flat £35,000 for her memoirs on condition that Edward's letters were handed over to King George. She had refused the offer, and now she asked for du Cros' advice.

I once more expressed the hope that she would never lend herself to this transaction, which would always remain a stigma on her name— once done it could never be undone—and advised her either to keep the letters or surrender them voluntarily herself and not through the medium of any third party or under pressure. L W assured me that this was the course she herself really wished to follow, but that she would take further time to consider it.

A week later du Cros had an unexpected visitor. Here is the last unexpected character to appear on the scene, the strangest of all and certainly a mysterious one. He claimed to be an American, gave the name of "Mr. Marsh" and said he was a friend of Lady Warwick. He asked the value of the Warwick estates. Du Cros told him "£250,000," after "Mr. Marsh" had explained that an American friend of his, British-born, had a wife with £500,000 of her own who was willing to gamble this sum to achieve the common American ambition of establishing herself at the top of the social ladder in England. She thought she might achieve this ambition by buying a big and noble estate. And by one other thing. This half-millionairess wanted to perform a direct loyal service to His Majesty King George. A condition of purchase of the Warwick estate would be that Lady Warwick should "surrender" certain letters known to be in her possession.

Du Cros told Lady Warwick about this visit. Her explanation of it was downright frightening. "Mr. Marsh's" friend, she declared, was "really a German with ulterior political motives."

This was too much. Even for du Cros it was too much. Agitatedly he went back to his friend Lord

Albemarle. They lunched together at the Marlborough Club on January 28, and after du Cros had told the whole story to the Earl he asked him to tell it to Stamfordham "so that I can drop out if he was indifferent."

Nothing was ever heard again of "Mr. Marsh" or the suspected "German agent." Nor, incidentally, about Frances Warwick's career as an agent in armament deals.

Meanwhile the Palace was proceeding in its legal machinations to silence the irritating Countess forever. The injunction granted in Chambers in July 1914 was, of course, not a conclusive victory for the Palace. That injunction was merely interlocutory. Granted, as an interlocutory injunction can be, on *prima facie* evidence—in this case, the affidavits from Viscount Knollys and Charles Russell—it did no more than *delay* Lady Warwick's professed intention of publishing the letters in America. The ultimate decision in the dispute had yet to be legally made. That decision, the Palace hoped, would be a judgment against her publishing, but judgment could be made only when the defendants had had an opportunity of stating their case before the judge at an adjourned hearing of the application.

For the hearing, more evidence had to be collected. That was why Russell gave du Cros his own affidavit and asked him to use it to guide him in writing for the King's solicitors a full statement on his part in the affair, recording everything Lady Warwick and Harris had said to him.

Du Cros wrote that statement. It is one of the documents in the pile before me. To it he left attached a sheet of notes to make clear certain points to anyone who might eventually read it. One of the points he makes is his explanation of why he let Frances Warwick read this statement. He "considered it right that Lady Warwick should see the statement he had made to the King's solicitors in order that she could not reproach him with acting unfairly towards her and to afford her every opportunity of replying." She did reply, as I have mentioned earlier, with occasional testy marginal comments and corrections.

But she also was in the process of writing a statement. As she was now a defendant in the injunction action in the King's Bench, she had had to resort to her lawyer, Sir Henry Paget-Cooke, senior partner in the law firm of Russell-Cooke and Company at 11 Old Square, Lincoln's Inn, London, and under Sir Henry's direction she was composing an affidavit giving her version of the affair and her account of all the interviews she had had with du Cros and Harris and the others involved.

By this time Frances Warwick was enraged and bitter. She felt that the Palace had played a dirty trick on her. She had hoped that the King or his family, the Royal Family, or his friends would have paid up quietly and nicely "like gentlemen." She had never dreamed that the King—he of all people—would be so unchivalrous as to go to law against a woman and a Countess.

But now at last she knew that her grand plan to extort money by threats of publishing had collapsed. One of the most valuable documents in the whole of the collected evidence on my desk is a statement she made as a supplement to her affidavit for Sir Henry. It beautifully illustrates her state of mind at the time, her anger and her realization of defeat. In it she is making a desperate attempt to reinstate herself, to clear herself from the imputation of having attempted blackmail. It is in line with what she wrote in those memoirs she did get down to writing many years later—a denial that she ever had any intention of telling the story of her love affair. But, knowing what we do know, having seen the evidence of the things she did in 1914 which she believed would never be disclosed, we can now recognize this statement only as a damning revelation of her deceitfulness. Yet it is written with such fervor, with such blazing sincerity, that one wonders if she had not almost convinced herself of her starry innocence. If we had no evidence other than this truly remarkable document, if we could read nothing but these two sheets of typescript signed "F. Warwick" and had never seen those letters of hers to du Cros or those other documents supporting, step by step, our history of her intrigue, we would be wholly convinced that she was a wronged woman.

To the end of his days, whenever he recalled reading this amazing outburst, du Cros never forgot the exasperated bewilderment he experienced when he saw Frances Warwick presenting herself as a guiltless woman ringed around with false friends who had uttered lying accusations against her. He was shocked by the vehemence with which she lashed out at the King's advisers for stooping so low as to go to law against a noblewoman on such an intimate matter as her friendship with dear Edward; but what surprised him most of all was to learn at this stage that she had never intended to publish Edward's letters. It was as though she had never told him or written to him of her plan to quote them in her memoirs; as though she had never shown them to Frank Harris at all, let alone negotiated with him about their value. Why, du Cros thought, if he had not had in his desk those letters of hers and his own blow-by-blow record of the interview at the Ritz, he could almost have believed it had all been nothing but a bizarre dream. Nor did she spare him. She made plain to him something that he ought to have appreciated from the moment she first approached him, that she had chosen him as a go-between because she judged he was just the kind of man who would jump at the chance of acting as an emissary to the King in the hope of thus earning some Royal favor.

Methodical as ever, du Cros filed this outburst away among the growing stack of "Darling Daisy" papers. I am glad that he did so and that I was able to unearth it. I can now admit that until I found and read this particular document it had been only a theory of mine that Frances Warwick had deliberately chosen du Cros as a likely agent for her purpose: the man who, in the hope of earning some advancement, would do just what she wanted —hurry off to the Palace with news of her threats. The document gave me the writer's joy of seeing what had been a supposition confirmed as undeniable fact.

Because of the order later made by the King's Bench Judge that a sealed envelope of documents in the case should be destroyed, we cannot know for certain whether du Cros passed a copy of Frances Warwick's outburst on to the solicitors. I do not think he would have. Perhaps he managed to persuade her that it could do her case great harm. In any case, he certainly felt it put him in a not too pleasant light, particularly as in this very period when Frances Warwick was molding herself into an attitude of righteous indignation he was having a little battle of his own with the King's solicitors. This tussle began in September 1914 when he heard that Viscount Helmsley, assistant private secretary to the First Lord of the Admiralty and a relative of Lady Warwick's, had been making critical and somewhat damaging comments—apparently within the precincts of the House of Commons—about Arthur du Cros and the part he had played in the affair.

Upset by this, du Cros asked Russell to write to Viscount Helmsley pointing out forcefully that everything du Cros had done had been done at the request of the King's solicitor and Lord Stamfordham. Hemsley "replied apologetically," and Russell sent the letter to du Cros. Du Cros did not keep it because, he explains in one written note, Russell promised to send him a further letter substantiating that du Cros "had acted throughout at the request of and on behalf of the King's advisers."

When this letter did not come, du Cros wrote to Russell reminding him of his promise. Such a letter, he pointed out, "might have been useful as a record to file with my papers." Du Cros got no reply, and at last, in February 1915, he tackled Albemarle about it. The actual letter he sent is unobtainable, but I have the heavily corrected draft on 14 Regent Street notepaper which he obviously handed to his typist. It reads:

Private. Feb 1/15.

I send you a copy of my letter to Russell, to which no reply was vouchsafed. His attitude became so suddenly and so unaccountably discourteous that I shall be interested to learn whether Lord Stamfordham is aware of what has taken

place or whether the whole affair has now be-
come a matter of indifference to him.

Albemarle, who was by then of course on military
duty, was apparently too busy to reply to this letter
for a fortnight. Or perhaps he had felt compelled to
consult Russell and find out what he ought to say to
du Cros. The reply, dated February 16, was written
on Albemarle's coroneted 39 Belgrave Square notepaper, but Albemarle crossed out that address and
wrote over it his wartime address: "Officers Guard
Room, Horse Guards, Whitehall. Telephone No. 11
War Office." In it he said he had seen Lord Stamfordham and suggested du Cros might come to his
office the following day. Then, to assure du Cros that
the Lady Warwick affair was as yet by no means
dead, he added: "The interest in the matter is
maintained."

Two days later du Cros did at last receive a letter
from Russell. It was marked "Strictly Personal and
Private," but it was not the "reference" that du Cros
had asked for. Russell gave two reasons to excuse
himself for not writing earlier. One was that, as du
Cros "had brought a solicitor on the scene," Russell
had concluded that du Cros did not want any direct
approach. (This referred to the fact that du Cros
had taken his Mr. Purchase with him the last time he
had gone to Russell's office.) The other reason for
not writing, Russell said, was that "there was really

nothing to communicate up to a few days ago."
Among the scribbled comments du Cros made on this
letter is one saying "These are not reasons which
should be given to explain a broken pledge. He
behaved with duplicity and ingratitude."

In his letter Russell offered to explain to du Cros
exactly how everything stood "any time you have
time to spare and are in this neighborhood." Against
which du Cros writes acidly, "But not in writing,
which might detract from his achievement. I declined
the offer."

The last comment contains the germ of this developing quarrel and is the reason why it has been
necessary to tell the story of this little side issue. Du
Cros was beginning to be angry that the part he had
played in the affair was not being recognized. He
did, perhaps justifiably, expect some return for all
he had done, and he felt that Russell was now
pushing him into the background. In another comment written elsewhere he repeats the complaint that
Russell never sent him a letter of thanks for his
services to the King. He writes that he still did not
know why Russell never sent that letter, but assumes
"that Russell wanted to stand in the limelight."
Then, in a moment of bitterness, he reveals his
innermost thoughts more openly. Of Russell he
writes, "*He* received a baronetcy."

It is not the only time he comments on that. Three
times in his notes he refers to Russell having been

made a baronet. One such comment reads: "Russell was created a Baronet!! A. du C. never received a line or word of thanks from anyone." So Lady Warwick had not been wrong. The du Cros she had chosen as her intermediary *had* been a man who expected that reward which she described in her statement as some "honour and distinction." But, then, what man would not expect it?

Having declined the offer of meeting Russell, du Cros wrote again, reminding the solicitor of his promise to write a letter. Russell replied, "My recollection is that you were anxious I should write some letter which would relieve some misapprehension under which a certain member of the House of Commons was under, and this I did." He could not, he said, remember any letter of du Cros' going unanswered.

Against which du Cros scribbles: "He did not overlook anything when he wanted my services. See his telegrams and telephone messages."

In his earlier letter Russell had attempted to end on a genial note and, after asking du Cros to drop in and hear the news, said that "the later developments have been rather amusing." In his next letter Russell writes: "I cannot very well in a letter explain what has happened, but it looks as if the incident were about to be terminated."

Indeed it was. In London a date was being fixed for the hearing of the adjourned injunction application. At Easton Lady Warwick was awaiting news in a frenzy of anxiety and anger.

On May 1, 1915 she wrote a violently threatening letter to du Cros. He was seriously disturbed by it and sent a message to the King's solicitors telling them that she was asking him to send her news immediately about any decision that might be made in Chambers, because she intended, as soon as such a decision was made, to publish her own story in full of the abominable way she had been dealt with and insulted by the Royal solicitors. She intended, apparently, to publish it in the United States and obviously expected Harris to write it. What was more, du Cros went on, she was claiming her rights as a peeress and the wife of a peer to demand an audience with the King to confront him in person and tell him just what she thought of the whole affair.

But her own lawyer, Sir Henry Paget-Cooke, had to tell her that the Palace were bound to win the case and nothing could be gained by trying to exact revenge. In fact, he told her that now she must do what she could to salvage her reputation. She could do this by offering to surrender the letters to King George without conditions or threats, and at last she had to agree that this was her only course.

A romantic story eventually got around, even among the du Cros family and other people closely associated with the affair, describing melodramatic circumstances in which the letters were at last handed to King George. The story goes that a private rendezvous was arranged between the King and Frances Warwick a certain distance down The Mall from Buckingham Palace. The time was to be night. Lady Warwick was to drive up in one car and the King drive down in another. When the cars met, Lady Warwick was to hand over to her sovereign the letters his father, her lover, had written to her. It is a pity one must destroy that story. Such an incident would not have been out of character with all the bizarre events of the intrigue.

But it didn't happen. For some reason or other, Lady Warwick was, despite all her insistence on her right to meet the King in private audience, not anxious to do so. In fact, on June 11, 1915, she wrote to du Cros asking him if he would again act as her intermediary, this time to take the package of letters to the King. She suggested to du Cros that his doing this might earn him some advancement.

That final remark suggests that even she had come round to thinking that poor du Cros deserved some reward, even if nothing more than a bit of the limelight. Or was she just being kind to him, softening the blow of the staggering financial burden this "Darling Daisy" affair was shortly going to inflict on the loyal liege.

However, du Cros flatly refused to carry "the parcel" to his sovereign. He wired her at Easton:

STILL THINK YOUR INTERESTS WOULD BE
BEST SERVED BY ACTING YOURSELF AND
NOT THROUGH AN INTERMEDIARY WOULD
LIKE SEE YOU MONDAY AFTER SIX IF
CONVENIENT

Perhaps it was Frances herself who fabricated that legend of the meeting in The Mall. Such a romantic story would be characteristic of her, but the truth is very different. When du Cros refused her suggestion that he should take the letters to the King, she asked her lawyers to deal with them in the way they thought best. In the early stages of the action she, her husband and Bruce Logan had all been represented by the same solicitors, Messrs. J. D. Langton and Passmore, but, according to the Cause Book of the King's Bench Division, the Earl and Countess, about one month prior to the settlement, changed their solicitors to the firm of Messrs. Russell-Cooke, of which the senior partner was Sir Henry Paget-Cooke. Frank Harris was represented by Oliver Richards and Parker of Warwick Street, London W. 1.

It appears that Sir Henry advised Lady Warwick to entrust the letters to him, for on June 14, 1915,

(*253*)

when the adjourned application came before Mr. Justice Low, Sir Henry wrote to her at Dunmow:

The Judge was very amenable when he heard that you had undertaken to hand the letters to me, and ultimately adjourned the proceedings until the 5th proximo pending the receipt of the letters.

I stated that I was not prepared to hand them over to Mr Russell, but that I would do so to either Viscount Knollys or Sir Arthur Davidson.

On July 5, 1915, the battle ended. On that day the adjourned application for the injunction came again before Mr. Justice Low. The Right Honorable H.E. Duke, K.C., and Mr. McCardie appeared for the plaintiffs. Mr. Alderson Foote, K.C., and Mr. Harold Morris appeared for Lady Warwick and her associates. That July 5 is not only memorable in the story of the "Darling Daisy" affair but also remarkable in the story of British law, for in court that day happened something which is surely unique in legal history.

Mr. Justice Low played his part in helping the Palace not only to silence Lady Warwick but to stamp into the ground all evidence of the "Darling Daisy" affair in an attempt to make it impossible that the story could ever be told.

The Judge made an order staying the action until

further notice, but he also decreed that the documents contained in a sealed envelope and deposited in court should be handed over to Sir Henry Paget-Cooke "forthwith to be destroyed by him." What were those documents? Lawyers studying the meager records of the case on my behalf have suggested that they were Edward's love letters to Lady Warwick. For my part, I find it difficult to believe that the Palace would have asked for such priceless documents to be destroyed and that the sealed envelope contained other papers connected with the case. Edward's letters would surely have been retrieved by the Royal Family and preserved in the archives of family papers. Even the story of the meeting in The Mall is easier to believe than that the Royal Family would have had Edward's letters destroyed.

However, one thing is certain. Stamfordham and Russell were determined that not one scrap of "Darling Daisy" evidence should be left around, and surely the most amazing feature of Mr. Justice Low's order is the direction that *all the affidavits filed in the action should be taken off the file of the court* and returned to the solicitors for the parties who had filed them.

An eminent lawyer has since expressed the opinion that such an order is, at the least, "highly unusual, if not unprecedented," demonstrating the influence the Establishment could exert even on the judicature fifty years ago. It was a deliberate and perhaps even unconstitutional act designed to remove from the public domain documents which might at some future date reveal details of the "Darling Daisy" battle, and is the reason why an exhaustive search of the Public Records Office yielded virtually no details of the affair. Not until I realized this did I appreciate the unique value of the documents unearthed in Switzerland. Had Arthur du Cros not preserved every scrap of paper so meticulously, the Darling Daisy story could never have been told.

Because of its unique character I present Mr. Justice Low's order in full:

IN THE HIGH COURT OF JUSTICE

1914 P. No. 1594

KING'S BENCH DIVISION

MR. JUSTICE LOW

BETWEEN THE RIGHT HONOURABLE SIR DIGHTON MACNAGHTEN PROBYN, THE RIGHT HONOURABLE THE VISCOUNT KNOLLYS AND COLONEL SIR ARTHUR DAVIDSON

Plaintiffs

and

BRUCE LOGAN, THE RIGHT HONOURABLE FRANCES EVELYN COUNTESS OF WARWICK, THE RIGHT HONOURABLE FRANCIS RICHARD CHARLES GUY GREVILLE EARL OF WARWICK AND FRANK HARRIS

Defendants

UPON HEARING *the Solicitors for the Plaintiffs and for the Defendant the Right Honourable Frances Evelyn Countess of Warwick* IT IS ORDERED *that all further proceedings in this Action be stayed until further Order and that there be no Order on the Summons dated 18th. February, 1915, except that the documents contained in a sealed envelope deposited in Court in this Action and indorsed "In the High Court of Justice King's Bench Division Probyn v Logan 1914 P. No. 1594" be handed out to Sir Henry Paget Cooke the said Defendant's Solicitor forthwith to be destroyed by him. All affidavits filed in this action by any of the parties to be taken off the File of the Court and returned to the present Solicitors for the parties who filed them respectively.*

That was the end.

Lady Warwick was gagged at last, Charles Russell could close his "Darling Daisy" file, and the King and Stamfordham could turn their whole attention to the pressing duties of getting on with the war without the nagging fear that at any moment a Royal scandal would burst into print and discredit throne, government and nation.

As soon as she had received Sir Henry's letter, Frances Warwick wrote to du Cros. This letter is the last of the letters in the collection uncovered in

Switzerland. Indeed an appropriate last letter, for it brought the wheel full circle, recalling to du Cros the very argument she had expressed at the beginning of the affair: that it was Edward and the glittering social crowd clustered around him and the lavish hospitality he had demanded which had plunged her into debt and eventually reduced her to trying to make money out of the confidences of a love affair.

Well, she was now saved from that shameful course. Freed from her debts, she could now devote herself to a life of good works at Easton—such things as writing her autobiographies (without Edward's letters, of course, and indeed without even a claim that he had been her lover) and also a novel with the teasing title of *The Prime Minister's Pyjamas*, as well as grooming herself into so typical an English countrywoman that eventually when she was giving details of her life to *Who's Who* she was able to list as her recreations only such proper and ladylike pursuits as gardening, riding and driving horses, the welfare of all animals and birds, and reading.

In this valedictory letter to du Cros she freely admitted that she was deeply indebted to him for her release into a new untroubled life.

What was the reason for this quite moving expression of gratitude to a man whom only a few months ago she had been threatening to expose in further chapters of her memoirs? There was ample reason. By his own generosity Arthur du Cros had put Frances Warwick in a fairly safe position financially. He had agreed that the dividends due to him should revert to her as part of her income. He had also agreed that he would not press for payment of the principal during her lifetime. This promise he had given only verbally, but, as he records in a note years later, the promise was "subsequently faithfully acted upon." But he had done even more for her. He had done that very thing she had obliquely suggested to him on the day they came back from France together. He had taken upon his own shoulders those outstanding bills of £48,000, with the result that she now owed him at least £64,000. So that amount was what she really got after all for "dear Edward's" letters. Nothing from the Royal Family, nothing from American publishers, but a nice £64,000 from her intermediary, Arthur du Cros.

He never got that £64,000 back. He got some of it. He records that "An anonymous friend repaid £7,500 in 1934." But he himself bore the rest of the burden, managing to spread it among the companies he owned, and makes mention of having canceled a "debt of £34,000 or thereabouts."

So Lady Warwick did not come out of the affair too badly. After all, £64,000 was not a vast amount below what she had been trying to get, apart from the amount she had promised to pay Frank Harris for his work. What did he get? There is no record anywhere that he got anything. It is likely he never saw a penny.

But not much sympathy need be wasted on Harris. Even tolerant Paris had got weary of him, and when the French police became too interested in his activities he had been forced into a humiliating retreat to England. He fled from Paris with his wife, Nellie, and two valises, and he found a refuge with Lady Warwick at Easton.

Lady Warwick had many famous tenants on her Easton estate. Among them were the composer Gustav Holst and the writer Philip Guedalla, but her most famous was the tenant of the house Easton Glebe. This was H. G. Wells, and he it is who throws some light on the last stages of the collaboration between Frances Warwick and Frank Harris. In his *Experiment in Autobiography* Wells recalls that one morning during the war, sometime in 1915, Lady Warwick "came sailing down from Easton Lodge to Easton Glebe" and asked him point-blank, "Why does Frank Harris say I am not to tell you he is here?"

Wells suggested that Harris—who had now thrown himself upon Lady Warwick's "never failing generosity"—was scared of being denounced and arrested as a traitor. In Paris he had been boasting too much about his German sympathies and "his influence with Indian Princes." However, Harris emerged from "hiding" eventually and met Wells in Frances Warwick's company.

"Harris, a very subdued Harris, brightened up," says Wells, "and we did what we could to make his stay in Essex pleasant until he could get a passage to America. He sat at my table and talked of Shakespeare, Dryden, Carlyle, Jesus Christ, Confucius and other great figures."

Soon, however, Harris set off for America. Just after he had gone Frances Warwick, walking with Wells in his rose garden at Easton Glebe, told him that she had shown Harris "a number of highly confidential letters from a certain Royal person."

"You did not give them to him?" Wells asked.

"Oh, no, but he asked to look through them. He thought he might advise me about them. One doesn't care to destroy things like that. They have historical importance."

"And are they now in his valise on their way to America?" Wells asked.

Lady Warwick might have thought Wells was talking about copies of the letters, or maybe she was, as ever, trying to dramatize a situation, for she asked Wells, "How did you know that?"

"Ah, well," Wells said philosophically, "even if the ship is torpedoed, Harris will stick to those letters."

Actually the ship Harris traveled on was twice alerted to take precaution against enemy action and on one occasion a torpedo attack seemed imminent. But Harris arrived safely in New York and wrote to Lady Warwick to tell her he was there and would continue his work on her behalf. Wells writes that some sum of money *was* paid to Harris to recover the letters and place them in discreet hands, but this is almost certainly untrue and may have arisen from some other yarn of Lady Warwick's.

A year later, in 1916, Arthur du Cros at last received that same honor for which he had so much envied the solicitor Russell—a baronetcy. But it would be unfair not to record that after the "Darling Daisy" affair he rendered his country and his King service far more meritorious and outstanding than frustrating blackmail and paying "hush money." He showed once again his enthusiasm for motor vehicles by initiating Britain's first Motor Ambulance Movement in 1914, subscribing £80,000 for the purchase of the first three ambulances and financing them throughout the war. He also gave £7,000 to the London School of Medicine for Women at the Royal Free Hospital.

In 1929, only seven months before the Clarence Hatry crash robbed him of millions, he performed a personal service to his sovereign, lending Craigweil, the big mansion he had bought at Aldwick near Bognor, to King George for his convalescence after a dangerous illness. The King arrived there by ambulance on February 9, 1929, and by the following morning Queen Mary, who had come down ahead in her own car to receive him, was busily superintending the cutting down of the ivy that du Cros' sons had encouraged to grow over the face of the house in the hope of hiding architecture which they had never found admirable. Queen Mary was always famed as a cutter-down of ivy, which, she argued, harbored damp and spoiled buildings. But she liked Craigweil, describing it as "nice and convenient and close to the sea," and in March her favorite grandchild, the present Queen, then nearly three, came to stay there with her nurse, and Queen Mary recorded in her diary, "I played with Lilibet in the garden making sand pies! The Archbishop of Canterbury came to see us." King George stayed in du Cros' house for fourteen weeks, and in recognition of his restoration to health while he was there the town of Bognor was allowed to adopt its present name of Bognor Regis.

When du Cros, still suffering from the Hatry disaster, put Craigweil and its contents up for auction in 1932, it was revealed that he had made his home a treasure house. Among the pictures, miniatures, statuary, porcelain and a wealth of antique furniture offered for sale during the five-day auction were paintings attributed to El Greco, Rembrandt, Raphael, Velásquez, Turner, Constable, Gainsborough and many other masters.

Meanwhile Lady Warwick continued her climb to

popular favor as a great and distinguished Socialist Peeress. Easton Lodge became more and more the haven of Socialists and trade-unionists, and eventually she offered Easton Lodge, the home she had said was her only "love," to the Trades Union Congress to be converted into a college for the Socialist movement. The ceremony of handing over was actually performed, but the General Strike in 1926 caused the project to be abandoned.

Three years before that she had appeared as a Socialist candidate for Parliament. She fought the Parliamentary division of Warwick and Leamington against Mr. Anthony Eden, then a markedly handsome twenty-five-year-old Tory. Eden had married the stepdaughter of Frances Warwick's daughter. His sister had married her eldest son, the one she had named Leopold after the Prince she might have married.

In one election speech she assured her audience that, although she was a Countess of ancient family, she was "very poor." Sadly she added, "The young and thoughtless woman who lived at Warwick Castle in the old days is no more." Despite this assurance and despite her territorial influence in the Warwick area, Eden won the election, later became one of the great hopes of the Tory Party as Foreign Secretary and Winston Churchill's right-hand man in the House of Commons, but finished his political career as the disastrous "Suez Affair" Premier.

Frances, Countess of Warwick, died on July 26, 1938, aged seventy-seven. To Nancy Galpin, her housekeeper at Easton Lodge for eighteen years, she left, "for unfailing devotion and disinterested loyalty," an annuity of £400 and trunks full of the clothes she had worn in her glittering heyday as a hostess, as well as her pet dogs and birds. The birds were an embarrassing legacy for poor Nancy Galpin. There were no fewer than five hundred of them.

"I fear the dear Countess did not know that it costs £8 a week to feed them," she said, and sent more than two hundred budgerigars and canaries to the Royal Society for the Prevention of Cruelty to Animals at East Molesey in Surrey.

"A thousand times," she added, "I have asked myself 'Will her ladyship be annoyed with me?' But I simply cannot keep all the birds. There is the cost of the food and the man's wages, and I am moving to a little house on the estate where there is room for only a small aviary.

"I am taking one hundred of the birds—the ones her ladyship loved most—with me. You see, I have also her ladyship's thirteen dogs to look after. Those cost me £2 a week as well as twenty-five shillings for the widow woman who helps me to look after them."

So ends the story of Frances Warwick, once the chosen bride for a Prince of the Blood Royal, wife of an Earl, lover of an Irish sailor and a Prince of Wales, and first Socialist noblewoman. Also, an unsuccessful blackmailer of the Royal Family. That last enterprise of hers was her least creditable and most hurtful, but the man most injured by it, Arthur du Cros, eventually forgave her. This is proved by one of his scribblings on the "Darling Daisy" documents, perhaps a comment he made on the very day when he collected the papers into one bundle to hide them away. He wrote: "Harris was the moving spirit." Obviously du Cros had come round to thinking that the rascally journalist was the real evil genius behind the whole sorry intrigue.

In which case the final words Frances Warwick wrote to du Cros on the affair must have illustrated to him the accidental way in which destinies can be decided and lives come full circle. For just after she had signed this last letter to him Frances Warwick suddenly thought of something she had never before deemed worth telling him. So in a P.S., framed in such words that one imagines she was smiling mischievously over the aptness of it all, she told du Cros that it was Edward himself, dear, dear Edward, who, at a party at the house of Lady Dorothy Nevill, first introduced her to Frank Harris.

Surely we could not find a more exquisitely perfect footnote for the whole "Darling Daisy" story. Though if Frances Warwick herself were asked, she would most likely choose for the final words of this history four lines of a poem by Dryden which was, she claimed, her favorite piece of poetry:

Be fair or foul, or rain or shine,
The joys I have possessed, in spite of fate, are
mine.
Not heaven itself upon the past has power;
But what has been, has been, and I have had my
hour.

Index

27.V.94

THEO LANG

Born in Bradford, Yorkshire, England, Theo
Lang left school at fifteen to earn his own
living, worked for a time as a farmer's boy on
the Yorkshire moors and eventually became
a newspaper executive. At one time he maintained a castle in Scotland (writing in the
very room Mary Queen of Scots occupied during her third honeymoon), a penthouse in
London and a villa in Italy. He has since re-
trenched and now has "nothing more than the
top half of a peasant house on the Sorrento
peninsula with a wide, shabby terrace hanging
over the Mediterranean." He commutes several times a year by car between Naples and
London and still does an enormous amount of
newspaper work, contributing regularly to
Britain's *Sunday Mirror* and writing special
features for magazines and other newspapers.
He wrote his first novel on a guardroom table
while in the British Army. He has since
written nine other books and edited four volumes in a definitive series on *The Queen's
Scotland*. Mr. Lang is now at work on a book
of history and a novel.